CARIBBEAN
VEGAN

THE EXPERIMENT

BECAUSE EVERY BOOK IS A TEST OF NEW IDEAS

CARIBBEAN
VEGAN

CARIBBEAN
VEGAN

MEAT-FREE,

EGG-FREE,

DAIRY-FREE

Authentic

Island Cuisine

for Every

Occasion

TAYMER MASON

CARIBBEAN VEGAN: *Meat-Free, Egg-Free, Dairy-Free*
Authentic Island Cuisine for Every Occasion

The Experiment, LLC
260 Fifth Avenue
New York, NY 10001-6425
www.theexperimentpublishing.com

This book contains the opinions and ideas of its author. It is intended to provide helpful and informative material on the subjects addressed in the book. It is sold with the understanding that the author and the publisher are not engaged in rendering medical, health, or any other kind of personal professional services in the book. The author and publisher specifically disclaim all responsibility for any liability, loss, or risk—personal or otherwise—which is incurred as a consequence, directly or indirectly, of the use and application of any of the contents of this book.

Many of the designations used by manufacturers and sellers to distinguish their products are claimed as trademarks. Where those designations appear in this book and The Experiment was aware of a trademark claim, the designations have been capitalized.

The Experiment's books are available at special discounts when purchased in bulk for premiums and sales promotions as well as for fundraising or educational use. For details, contact us at info@theexperimentpublishing.com.

Library of Congress Control Number: 2010924686

ISBN 978-1-61519-025-6

Cover design by Susi Oberhelman
Cover photographs by Cynthia Nelson
Author photograph by Jean Jarreau
Photo insert food styling and photography by Cynthia Nelson
Text design by Pauline Neuwirth, Neuwirth & Associates, Inc.

Manufactured in the United States of America
First published November 2010
Published simultaneously in Canada

10 9 8 7 6 5 4 3 2 1

To Cecelia, Ricardo, Richie, and Daniel with love

CONTENTS

Note: 📷 indicates that the recipe is pictured in the photo insert.

CARIBBEAN
VEGAN

Note:  indicates that the recipe or ingredient is pictured in the photo insert.

INTRODUCTION

ONE OF THE biggest challenges I faced in writing this book was finding a way to convince people who live outside the Caribbean that they could eat authentic Caribbean food made with ingredients from their local supermarket. Caribbean cuisine is still one of the most unknown cuisines in the mainstream media. Documentaries depicting Caribbean food tend to focus on images of pineapples, coconuts, fish, and an array of unknown ingredients. But Caribbean cuisine is not all fruits and coconuts. It is a complex cuisine influenced by the many cultures that have played a role in this region: indigenous, African, French, Spanish, British, and more, including Indian, as the British brought many Indians to the islands to work as indentured servants. In essence, Caribbean food is a potpourri of flavors that has evolved over the years into a sophisticated, yet so far underappreciated, cuisine. In this book, I focus on foods from Barbados, Saint Lucia, Trinidad and Tobago, Jamaica, Grenada, and the French West Indies, as well as Guyana, which is in South America.

Because I wanted to be sure that most of the recipes could be made anywhere in the world, I used a team of twenty testers from all over the world. Many of the testers said the project helped them rediscover their hometowns. Ethnic markets that they had never ventured into became their favorite haunts, and they got to know some vegetables from their regular supermarkets that they had never used before.

Vegans do not eat meat, fish, poultry, eggs, dairy products or honey—basically, any food made from animal products. Many vegans also do not wear leather, fur, wool, or silk as these fabrics are obtained from animals. Most vegans are vegans because they have compassion for animals, and they do not want to contribute to animal suffering. Many people believe that vegans eat this way primarily for the health benefits, but eating compassionately is a primary motivation for many vegans.

Do not confuse vegan Caribbean food with Ital food, also known as vital food, eaten by the Rastafarian community. However, vegan Caribbean food can be Ital, and many of the recipes in this book can be adapted to fit into a Rastafarian diet. There are many different groups of Rastafarians, and orthodox Rastafarians may follow strict rules regarding the type of utensils used and cooking without salt. One technique that defines Ital food is cooking in coconut milk that is reduced to oil. Avoid associating Rastafarianism with veganism, even if it does employ vegan food. Ital food is about a way of eating, while veganism is about ethics and eating. In addition, some Rastafarians eat fish, further distinguishing the two. Vegan Caribbean cuisine makes use of existing vegan dishes in traditional Caribbean cuisine and also takes existing Caribbean recipes and "veganizes" them.

You may be wondering how a Caribbean girl like me became vegan. I wish I could tell you a heroic story of how I saw an animal being mistreated and decided to change my ways, but it did not happen like that. You see, I was interning as a food microbiologist/technologist in a food processing plant in Barbados. One day I was showing my boss how to make British pork pies, and we made many variations. I took home a couple of pies and gorged on them. Later that night, I became very sick—so sick that even to this day I can remember that night. When I woke up the next morning, I declared myself vegan, leaving my mother asking me, with a concerned look on her face, "So what will you eat for breakfast now?" I went back to work the next day and I told my boss I just went vegan. With his dry British humor, he asked, "What happened to the pork pies?" My boss was very supportive of my choice and I was excused from some work tasks, such as taste testing the meat products, but many of my co-workers still did not know I was vegan. But with time, people began to notice what I was bringing to work for lunch. They started asking questions, and finally I came out of the closet and told a bunch of meat-loving factory workers that I was vegan. I continued interning there, but as time went on, my focus was on expanding their existing vegetarian line. Eventually, upon completion of my university degree, I left the job. As my ethics against eating meat became stronger, it was time to move on.

How did my family and friends take it? Surprisingly, my dad decided to join me in the journey toward veganism, and he is still vegan. My mom, although not vegan, was very supportive and cooked me balanced vegan meals throughout my stressful university years in Barbados. I was always swamped with assignments and never had the time to cook, so my mother started making seitan chilies and green banana mash for me. Many of my peers did not understand why I would do this, and they often condemned me for going vegan, saying it was not really Caribbean to eat this way, that it was an eating fad of North America and Europe. I always received strange looks when I whipped out my homemade veggie burgers and my tofu scramble. It was not a good time for me. I did have some friends who stood by me and came over to try the new things I was making. They have been an important source of support in the writing of this book. Last but not least is my husband, a ten-year vegetarian who went vegan a year ago. When he was not cracking coconuts and helping me grate them, he was picking up stock for me that I always absentmindedly forgot to put on the grocery list.

I started cooking at the age fourteen because my aunt used to taunt me with the phrase "Hand full o' gold, can't wash a bowl." It basically means stuck-up, fussy, modern-day Caribbean girls cannot do anything in the kitchen. I loved my aunt, and I was also bent on proving her wrong and showing that I could be top dog in the kitchen. I was like a sponge, soaking up everything my parents, my grandparents, and TV chefs did in the kitchen. Eventually, after many years of developing my cooking repertoire, I was able to create my own signature style of cooking. My style is Caribbean comfort food, full flavored and slightly spicy with many Indo-Caribbean influences. My quest is to enlighten others about how this type of cuisine can fit into contemporary, modern-day homes around the world. Today, my aunt is really proud of this project and no longer taunts me with those words.

SOME NOTES ON CARIBBEAN COOKING

Caribbean cuisine has been influenced by many cultures and combines interesting textures and bold flavors ranging from sweet to spicy to a bit of both. Sadly, our cuisine has been and continues to be misrepresented and often neglected. I hope to shatter misconceptions about Caribbean cuisine, including that a dish is tropical simply because it contains a bit of pineapple or coconut. In this introduction, I will discuss some of the ingredients that give Caribbean food its unmistakable character. I will also discuss ingredients that may be mysterious to those unfamiliar with vegan cooking.

Caribbean Vegan contains authentic recipes eaten by people in the Caribbean on a daily basis, adapted for vegans. It also offers valuable information about cooking methods and the history of various Caribbean foods. Along the way, I will take you island-hopping as I share information about different culinary destinations.

You may be asking yourself what you can gain from this book. You will be gaining a new and delicious experience in the kitchen as you start cooking Caribbean-style.

You can make many Caribbean seasoning blends in your own kitchen, and I encourage you to do it, as they are an important part of the authenticity of the dishes. You will learn to use familiar herbs and spices in a different way. You will learn to use coconut and pineapple in tried-and-tested Caribbean desserts and savory dishes. You will be able to understand some of the historical links that make the foods of each island unique. Finally, you will come to understand Caribbean food in terms of flavor profiles so that you can come up with new recipes on your own.

Condiments appear first in this book because some of them are essential ingredients in many of the recipes. These condiments are easy to make, and most can be stored in a jar in the fridge for a long time. I suggest making the Bajan Seasoning (page 19), Bajan Pepper Sauce (page 23), and Caribbean Caramel (page 25) as your first recipes, as they are used most often. Everyday Vegan "Ham" (page 100) is another go-to recipe in this book.

A few important general notes:

- If no size is indicated for produce items in ingredients lists, assume that they're medium size.
- The same is true of pots, pans, and bowls; if size isn't indicated, medium should work just fine.
- For green onions (scallions), use both the white and green parts unless otherwise specified. For other onions, I usually use yellow or white. Either works just fine.
- Some of the recipes have long lists of ingredients. Do not be intimidated. Many of the ingredients are seasonings or condiments that only need to be measured out, so they are not time-consuming to prepare.

GLOSSARY OF INGREDIENTS

Here, I explain some of the unfamiliar ingredients in this book, with information on where to find them or how to prepare them, if appropriate. This glossary will also give you a good idea of some of the other names for the ethnic vegetables and other ingredients called for in this book. If you are not sure about a name, try an Internet search, or contact me via my blog Vegan in the Sun. And speaking of the Internet, if you discover that you cannot find some of the ingredients this book calls for at your local markets, look for them on the Web. Other than fresh ingredients, many are available from online vendors.

ADOBO SEASONING.   A dry seasoning salt common in Latino cuisine, adobo seasoning is usually a mixture of garlic and onion powder, oregano, and sometimes black pepper. Excellent substitutes include a vegetarian boullion cube or a seasoning salt of your choice.

ALMOND ESSENCE. Almond essence is a cheaper alternative to almond extract. It is most commonly found in the Caribbean as it is manufactured in many islands in the region. Feel free to use almond extract in the place of essence. Because essence is a little weaker in flavor than extract I suggest using half as much extract in any recipe that calls for almond essence.

ANGOSTURA BITTERS. A wide variety of bitters are available, but I typically use Angostura bitters in my drink mixes, desserts, and sauces. It is often an optional ingredient, but its flavor is worth getting used to. Angostura bitters, made from a variety of herbs, spices, and other ingredients, was initially manufactured as a medicine to cure upset stomach, but now it is found in most Caribbean kitchens. It is a necessity in making authentic Caribbean cocktails.

ANNATTO. Also called *roucou*, annatto is used as a natural coloring agent. To make what is known as red oil, cook about 1 part annatto seeds in 4 parts oil over medium heat. In the French West Indies this is typically made with palm oil and is known as *beurre rouge*, (French for "red butter, but not to be confused with classic *beurre rouge*, made with butter and red wine). Red oil is used as a coloring agent in French West Indian cuisine. It can also be used in place of saffron.

ARROWROOT. Arrowroot is a plant cultivated on some Caribbean islands, including Saint Martin and Saint Vincent. Its rhizome is processed to make a flour with a neutral flavor that works well as a thickening and binding agent in vegan desserts and sauces. Note that arrowroot flour is sometimes sold under the name arrowroot powder.

BOUQUET GARNI. This is a French term for a bundle of herbs cooked in a liquid or broth to add flavor. You can tie the herbs together with kitchen twine, or wrap them loosely in cheesecloth and tie the corners together. The bouquet garni is removed and discarded before serving the dish.

BRAGG LIQUID AMINOS. A popular condiment that is used by vegetarians and vegans, liquid amino acids provide the essential amino acids which are also found in protein. Note that it is not an amino acid substitute, since vegans can get all of the amino acids by eating balanced meals with complex carbohydrates. It is a good substitute for soy sauce and is excellent in tofu scrambles.

BREADFRUIT. Breadfruit was brought to the Caribbean in 1791 by Captain Bligh on the HMS *Bounty* to feed indentured servants and African slaves on the islands. There are reports that he brought it from the Philippines. Why would he do this? Well, breadfruit, a large, starchy, fruit with a green skin and white or yellow flesh, is very cheap to grow; once the tree is planted, it needs no additional tending and each tree can produce a lot of fruit. Breadfruit is also rich in vitamin C and provides high-energy starch, and you need all the energy you can get when you have to be cutting sugarcane all day, right? Breadfruit is a common food in the French West Indies and former colonies of France. It can be fried or roasted, boiled in soups, or mashed with margarine and nondairy milk to make Breadfruit Cou-Cou (page 151). Fresh breadfruit may be available in Asian and Latin American markets in the summertime. Depending on the recipe, you may be able to substitute canned breadfruit. (See photo insert, page 1.)

BROWNING. There is a recipe for browning in this book (Caribbean Caramel, page 25), but you can also buy this ingredient ready-made in most West Indian markets and the spice section of supermarkets with extensive ethnic food sections, usually labeled "browning" or "coloring." It is simply burnt sugar with a little water that is used to give a natural brown color to stews and some cakes. Browning is used in small quantities only, as too much can make the dish quite bitter and overly dark in color.

CALABAZA SQUASH. In the Caribbean, calabaza squash is commonly referred to as pumpkin. Sometimes it is also called West Indian pumpkin. The size of this squash varies greatly, but it is often very large, so it is usually sold cut. In most recipes, you can substitute kabocha squash, or any other winter squash.

CASSAVA. Also called yuca and manioc, this is a large, long, very hard starchy root vegetable that is cultivated on most Caribbean islands. The skin color varies from a dark brown varnished appearance to pale and chalky depending on the variety and the soil in which it is grown. Raw cassava contains a toxic compound and is only safe to eat after being fully cooked. A visual sign of adequately cooked cassava is a slight cracked appearance on the surface. When preparing cassava, cut it into manageable pieces and remove the fibrous string in the middle. Grated cassava is used to make pone, a popular flourless dessert. (See photo insert, page 1.)

CASSIA. Cassia is member of the same family as cinnamon and is widely available and sometimes packaged under the label cinnamon. You can substitute cinnamon for cassia, but note that cassia has a slightly stronger flavor than cinnamon.

CHRISTOPHENE. Often called cho-cho, and also called chayote (though outside the Caribbean, not in the Caribbean), christophene is a mild-flavored squash that is nice for steaming or stuffing.

CORNMEAL AND CORN FLOUR. Corn flour is more finely ground than fine corn-meal. In many recipes, the two are interchangeable. I use cornmeal for making Cou-Cou (page 122) and corn flour for Conkies (page 191) and breads. I tend to stick to the brand of cornmeal I grew up using, which is Indian Girl, but there are other brands of high-quality cornmeal on the market. Look for bright yel-low cornmeal or corn flour. I sometimes use millet flour, known as guinea corn flour in the Caribbean, in combination with cornmeal.

CURRY POWDER. In Caribbean cuisine we tend to use curry powder, not Thai-style curry pastes. Most of the recipes in the book were developed using Madras curry powders, primarily brands made in the Caribbean, but an Indian-style medium-hot Madras curry powder would do. Madras curry powder tends to be orange-yellow, though some have a green color. On occasion, I used Colombo curry powder, a mild curry powder from the French West Indies. Although it does not pack the heat like the Madras curry powder, it has a wonderful roasted flavor. If you cannot find Colombo you can use a mild Madras.

ENER-G EGG REPLACER. This powdered starch is used to replace eggs as a bind-ing agent in baked goods recipes. It is whisked with warm water before being added to recipes.

GLUTEN FLOUR. Gone are the days when I would wash flour to get a ball of gluten for seitan. These days you can buy gluten flour, sometimes labeled "vital wheat gluten flour," in most natural food stores or supermarkets. It is a good source of protein, but it is not suitable for people with celiac disease or gluten intolerance.

GREEN BANANAS. Not to be confused with plantains, these are simply unripe bananas with a dark green skin. Their flavor is not anything like ripe bananas but have their own unique flavor. They are a staple in Saint Lucian cuisine. They are usually peeled, then boiled in salted water. During the process, their color goes from white to pinkish brown or gray.

HEARTS OF PALM. Usually available in cans in salted water, hearts of palm are used in fritters in the French-speaking islands and some salad dishes in the Spanish-speaking islands. In this book, I use them in Hearts of Palm and Tofu Scramble (page 55) and Eggplant, Hearts of Palm, and Spinach Stew (page 153).

LIQUID SMOKE.   Liquid smoke, made by condensing smoke, is used to add a smoky flavor to food. Liquid smoke can be used in recipes that would traditionally contain smoked meat. All liquid smoke is not created equal, so start with a small amount and add more to taste. Some popular brands are Colgin and Haddon House. There are different flavors of liquid smoke including mesquite and hickory.

MARMITE AND VEGEMITE.   Marmite and Vegemite are two brands of spreadable sticky paste that is popular in Great Britain and New Zealand. I use this spread in the book as a substitute for beef extract when I am working with textured vegetable protein (TVP). Marmite is also a good source of vitamin B12.

MEAT SUBSTITUTES.   Some of the main-course dishes in this book use textured vegetable protein (TVP), seitan, and other meat substitutes. In most cases, you can use whatever meat substitute you prefer. If you do not like meat substitutes, you can use beans instead. My aim was to make the meals high in protein, so the servings for the bean stews may be a little larger than you are accustomed to eating. A couple of commercial meat substitutes that I recommend are Morningstar Farms Meal Starters Chik'n Strips and Butler Soy Curls, or TVP chunks or granules depending on the recipe.

MILD CHILES.   These are a variety of mild chilies that are used in the Caribbean. The common names vary from pimento or sweet capsicum to seasoned peppers or vegetarian peppers, but some hybrids give a distinct flavor of Scotch bonnet without the added heat. Because these mild chilies have a low water content, Hungarian wax peppers can be substituted for them.

NONDAIRY CREAMER.   Nondairy creamer is the main base for the vegan ice creams, desserts, and cream sauces in this book. Nondairy creamer is rice or soy milk with a higher quantity of fat. Those that are sugar-free work best in savory applications. Nondairy creamers can be found in health food stores or supermarkets.

NONHYDROGENATED MARGARINE.   When I was growing up I never ate butter—not because we could not afford it, but because margarine was more readily available. Many islands make their own margarine, which is loosely referred to as "butter." Currently, I use Earth Balance, a soy-free nonhydrogenated vegan margarine. Some margarines contain whey or milk solids, so read the labels closely before you buy.

NORI.   Nori is a Japanese edible seaweed species. It is usually sold as sheets under the name dried nori sheets, which are suitable for rolling sushi. To prepare nori for the recipes in this book, lightly toast it by holding it over an open flame, which will make it easy to crumble.

NUTRITIONAL YEAST FLAKES.   This is a deactived yeast that can be a good source of vitamin B12 if the particular brand is fortified with it. Nutritional yeast is popular in vegetarian and vegan cooking and can be added to soups and sauces. This healthful yeast complex is also used in vegan cheese sauces, as its flavor is slightly similar to cheese.

OKRA.   Called gumbo in the French West Indies and ladyfingers in other places, okra is a green vegetable with fuzzy skin. Although it is usually cooked, it can be consumed raw when it is young. Okra is a good source of calcium.

PEA FLOURS.   In this book there are a few recipes that call for chickpea flour or split pea flour. Chickpea flour can be purchased at natural food stores or larger supermarkets. If you have a choice of split pea flours, I tend to prefer yellow split pea flour over green in most recipes, as it does not color the final product too much. If you do not have split pea flour, you can make your own in a coffee grinder. If you live in a humid environment, toast the peas gently in a low oven for a few minutes to dry them out before grinding.

PIGEON PEAS.   Also known as gungo peas in Jamaica and *gandules* in the Spanish-speaking islands, pigeon peas are available canned, fresh, frozen, or dried. Each of these versions has a different flavor. Fresh or frozen pigeon peas give the true taste of the pea. Pigeon pea rice is a staple on most of the islands.

PLANTAINS.   Also known as *banana jaune* or *plátanos*, plantains look like large bananas. The plantains that grow in the Caribbean are bright yellow and sweeter than those from Mexico, which have darker skins. Plantains should always be cooked before eating. They can be steamed or boiled in the skin or peeled and fried. They are usually served as a side dish.

SCOTCH BONNET PEPPERS.   These are some of the hottest peppers in the world. They are cousins to habaneros, which can be used as a substitute. When working with these peppers and other hot peppers, remember that the seeds and membranes pack the most heat. Try to avoid touching the seeds and interior of the peppers. It is a good idea to wear gloves. For chopping, you can hold the pepper with a fork, instead of your hands. Scotch bonnets can be frozen whole, and this freezing process tends to cut down the heat factor a little.

SEITAN. Also known as "wheat meat," seitan is the protein from flour. Seitan is commercially available in most supermarkets and can be marinated and prepared like meat. Seitan cannot be consumed by persons with gluten intolerances. A good substitute for seitan is textured vegetable protein (TVP).

SOURSOP. Also known as guanabana, soursop is a tropical green fruit with a spiny exterior. The flesh is soft and cotton-light, with a strong, distinctive flavor. Soursop is used all over the Caribbean for tarts, punches, and ice creams.

SUGAR. I use multiple sugars in the book. For desserts that I want to have a light color, I generally use organic granulated sugar. For desserts where color isn't as important, I go with a light brown cane sugar from Guadeloupe or Barbados. In the United Kingdom, this sugar is labeled "Barbados amber sugar." You can use muscovado sugar in recipes where the darkness of the dish is not an issue. In developing the recipes, sometimes I wanted the flavor of brown sugar but also wanted the dish to have a lighter color. In those cases, I call for light brown sugar. If "light" isn't specified, you can use any type of brown sugar. Turbinado sugar, which has a coarse texture, is great for sprinkling on certain cakes and pastries.

📷 **SWEET POTATOES.** Also known as *batata*, sweet potatoes are white-, yellow-, or orange-fleshed tubers with a reddish brown, purple, or pink skin. In the Caribbean, the white-fleshed sweet potato is most commonly used, but in the French West Indies orange-fleshed sweet potatoes are used for some desserts. I prefer white-fleshed sweet potatoes because they are denser, so that is what I usually call for. However, you can substitute yellow-fleshed sweet potatoes. In markets, yellow-fleshed sweet potatoes are sometimes labeled "Japanese sweet potatoes." Although sweet potatoes have a thin skin, if they are old they can be very difficult to peel. They can be baked in their skin, or peeled, chopped into cubes, and boiled. See page 1 of the photo insert for a picture of the white-fleshed sweet potato.

TEXTURED VEGETABLE PROTEIN (TVP). Sold in dehydrated chunks or granules or sometimes sold refrigerated, textured vegetable protein can be rehydrated quickly, marinated, and prepared. To rehydrate, pour hot water to just cover the granules or chunks and leave for about ten minutes to soak; pour off any excess water and marinate as per the recipe instructions.

VANILLA ESSENCE.   See almond essence; all the same applies here.

YAMS.   Yams are a confusing vegetable for some people. True yams are from the genus *Disoscorea*. These tubers can reach up to one hundred pounds or be as small as one pound. Yams are not sweet and should not be confused with the "yams" typically sold in U.S. markets, which are sweet potatoes, not true yams. Adding to the confusion, yams may be mislabeled "white sweet potatoes" in some ethnic markets. Yams have a texture similar to English potatoes but a nuttier flavor. Yams should be peeled and boiled in salted water because this method of preparation guarantees the best texture of the cooked yam. Yams have a thick, rough skin but are easy to peel. When peeling yams, do so under water to reduce the minor itching they can cause. My favorite way to eat yams is mashed with coconut milk, grated onion, and salt, and topped with Creole Sauce (page 36). Cooked yams are not good cold or reheated as they tend to get hard.

WORCESTERSHIRE SAUCE.   Many Worcestershire sauces contain anchovy paste and therefore are not vegan. Some brands are vegan; it may take some time to find one, but you will. I tend to buy Caribbean-made Worcestershire sauces like Swiss and Angostura, so have a look in local ethnic markets for potential options. It is also usually available in natural food stores. I use Worcestershire sauce in stews and some soups to mask the flavor of soy products. It also gives a good flavor profile to sauces.

ESSENTIAL EQUIPMENT FOR A CARIBBEAN KITCHEN

Several people have asked me if they need any special equipment to cook Caribbean food. My answer is yes and no. Many special kitchen tools are used in the region, but these days most Caribbean homes have typical modern-day, international-style kitchens. Most of the recipes in this book do not require special equipment. There are just a few things that I would like to highlight that you will need when cooking from this book.

BOX GRATER.   A sturdy stainless steel box grater is essential for grating coconut and root vegetables. You will need one with four to six sides, including one that shreds very fine. Some food processors have an attachment disk that can be used to grate coconut finely, but the coconut needs to be sliced in smaller pieces before adding it to the food processor.

COU-COU STICK. A cou-cou stick (see page 123) looks like a miniature cricket bat. It is used to stir cou-cou and to get those pesky lumps out of your preparations. If you do not have one, do not despair. A strong wooden spoon can also do the job.

PASTRY BLENDER. This is useful not only for a Caribbean kitchen but for anyone wanting to make good pastries. The pastry blender I use is a handheld type that is U shaped. A pastry blender will help you mix flour and fat well for short crust pastries.

PASTRY BRUSH. This is a fine-tipped brush that is useful for glazing pastries and seitan.

TAWA. A *tawa* is a round griddle used in Indian cooking, primarily for flat breads such as roti. If you don't have a tawa, you can use a crepe pan or a cast-iron skillet. That's what I did before I had a tawa, and they worked perfectly for all of my roti recipes. (See photo insert, page 10, step 8.)

SOME BASIC TECHNIQUES IN THE CARIBBEAN KITCHEN

Most of the cooking techniques used in Caribbean kitchens are familiar. However, because you may be unsure how to prepare some of our unfamiliar ingredients, I will outline a few techniques here.

▶ How to Peel and Prepare Green Bananas or Plantains

When cooking green, unripe bananas, you need to remove the skin before steaming or boiling. Otherwise the banana flesh turns black and the skin imparts a slightly bitter taste to the flesh.

To peel a green banana, use a sharp paring knife and cut off the two ends of the banana. Score lengthwise down the banana in at least two places, being careful not to cut into the flesh. Slip your thumb under the incision and pull back the skin. It should come off in one piece. If the skin breaks, peel off any small leftover pieces of skin with a knife.

Green bananas are best steamed or boiled in shallow water, as these cooking methods help them retain their flavor. Cook them in moderately salted water. Ripe plantains can be steamed, baked, or boiled in the skin, as this will not alter their flavor too much.

► How to Knead Dough

Many recipes here call for kneading dough in a bowl. In the Caribbean we often knead dough in the bowl rather than on a countertop because we've long done so-and for numerous other reasons: It allows every last bit of flour and other ingredients to be incorporated into the dough, it is easier to get the proper circular kneading motion, and it keeps our counters clean. (And think about it, it's just doing by hand what a stand electric mixer does with a mechanical arm.)

► How to Make Short Crust Pastry

Short crust pastries are made throughout the Caribbean and filled with sweet and savory fillings. In this book, they are used in a variety of recipes, from Lentil Patties (page 110) to Pineapple Tarts (page 197) to Coconut Tart (page 198). You may be asking, why make pastry when you can buy it premade? Store-bought short crust pastry is never to my liking. It is always rolled too thin and only useful for pie crust. To get the taste and the texture as authentic as possible, it is a good idea to make your own crust and use high-quality ingredients. The end product will taste superior. Homemade short crust pastry can be prepared in five minutes and placed in the refrigerator until needed.

When I was at secondary school, I had a food and nutrition teacher who was fond of me but exacting. She would stand over me as I tried to perfect my pastry making techniques. I can still hear her telling me, "Hurry! You are working that dough too hard, Taymer." The key to pastry making is speed and a light touch. You must keep everything cold, because if you do not, the fat particles will melt, leaving you with stiff, dry pastry.

Here are some rules for making the best short crust pastry, some learned from my food and nutrition teacher, and some from my own experience.

1. Keep everything cold, even your bowl and pastry blender. The aim is to keep the fat in small, isolated, solid particles so they do not melt until the pastry is baked. This makes it flaky. If you work the fat particles into the flour too much or your ingredients are warm, your baked pastry will be hard.

2. Use a pastry blender. This is an inexpensive and indispensable kitchen utensil that blends flour and fat effectively for pastry making. Using the pastry blender converts the flour and fat to a mass that resembles bread crumbs. You can use two cold forks, but that tends to slow you down. You can also use your fingertips, but if you do, work quickly; otherwise your body heat will melt the fat.

3. Cut the fat into small pieces before rubbing in to the flour. This helps cut down on the time needed to work the fat into the flour.

4. The water should be ice-cold. Add it 1 tablespoon at a time and disperse it well. You should mix the water in the flour quickly but efficiently between each addition of water. The amount given in each recipe should be adequate. If the dough is too dry, do not add more than 1 tablespoon of extra liquid.

5. Mixing with a cold flat metal spatula is the most effective way to bring the dough together. You can use your hands to form the dough into a ball, but you need to work quickly; otherwise the heat in your hands will start to melt the fat inside the pastry. I usually give myself 20 seconds to get the dough ball together. For beginning pastry makers, 30 seconds to get the dough together is a good goal to aim for.

6. It is very important to chill the dough for at least 25 minutes before use. This further solidifies the fat particles that are locked in the dough.

7. Do not use the dough directly out of the refrigerator, especially if it was refrigerated for over an hour. Give the dough about 2 or 3 minutes to rest before rolling it out.

8. When rolling dough, try to avoid excessive flour on the work surface. I never use flour, but in some situations light flouring of the surface may help. Excess flour makes the finished pastry extremely hard, as the additional flour changes the ratio of fat to flour and the extra flour coats the pastry, thus hardening the surface.

9. Never flip pastry dough over. It is not pizza dough. This tends to make the pastry too warm. The less and faster you work with the pastry, the better.

10. Roll pastry in one direction. You can change starting points during rolling, since some areas will need more rolling to get them even, but keep rolling in the same direction regardless of your initial starting point.

11. Cut pastry dough using a chilled knife or cookie cutter. If filling a pie pan, fit it in and trim off any untidy edges or style the crust to suit your preferences.

12. Assembled pastries or pie crusts can be chilled before putting them into the oven.

13. Blind bake pie crusts before filling, especially if the filling is moist, like a tofu quiche. (*Blind baking* means prebaking the pastry without a filling.) Prick the crust with a fork to prevent the middle from expanding too much. Placing some parchment paper and then dried beans on the surface of the crust will also help it keep its shape while baking.

14. If you desire, you can brush a sugar-water mixture on pastries periodically during baking to create a glossy, almost varnished finish. Use about ¼ cup of sugar dissolved in 2 teaspoons of water.

15. Pastries should be allowed to cool for at least 20 minutes before serving.

▶ Coconut 101

I use fresh coconut in my recipes, and I want to be sure you understand what they are, how to crack them open without harming yourself, and how to make coconut milk. By "fresh coconut," I mean the brown hairy coconuts that you see in supermarkets or ethnic markets. The liquid inside of these coconuts is called coconut water, but if the coconuts were harvested a long time ago, there may not be a lot of liquid inside.

Green coconuts are immature—not fully ripened. They usually contain a gelatinous flesh called coconut jelly, along with coconut water. Depending on the age of the coconut when harvested, the jelly can range from translucent and soft to opaque, white, and hard, which works well in fruit salads.

For me, the easiest way to crack open a coconut is to place it in a plastic bag and smash it on a concrete surface away from all pets and people. This usually cracks the coconut into at least five manageable pieces.

The most difficult part for most people is to separate the coconut flesh from its shell, because the coconut seems almost fused with the shell. Patience is the key here. A paring knife works well. Slip it into the area between the tough thin brown skin and the shell and carefully wiggle it to release the coconut from the shell. Don't get frustrated; it will eventually release. If you have the time, you can refrigerate the coconut overnight. This makes it easier to separate the flesh from the shell.

Now you have pieces of coconut, but still with the tough thin brown skin. Removing it can be tedious. In some recipes I leave it on for visual appeal. It depends on personal preference.

For the recipes that call for coconut in this book, I recommend grating the coconut as finely as possible using a box grater unless otherwise indicated. I always tell people the finer, the better, especially for baked goods. Finely grated coconut blends into batters and doughs more easily.

To make coconut milk, you need 1 coconut, a relatively large bowl, 6 to 8 cups of water, and some cheesecloth. Here again, grating finely is preferable, as the increased surface area will result in more milk. Put the coconut in the bowl, pour in half of the water, and, with clean hands, mix the water and grated coconut together. You need to press the grated coconut and water together in your hands to effectively extract the milk. Wrap some of the mixture in the cheesecloth, and squeeze out the liquid into a separate bowl. This is your coconut milk. Squeeze the coconut milk out of all of the pulp, and return the pulp to the bowl. Add the remaining water and repeat the process.

CONDIMENTS
AND SAUCES

HAVE YOU EVER wondered how Caribbean food gets those distinct flavor notes that you can't put your finger on? It comes from wet seasoning blends that are used to flavor the food. These blends, which were used to preserve food in the days before refrigeration, are used extensively in all households in the region. Wet seasonings play a valuable role in enhancing the flavor of sauces and soups and can also be added to tofu scrambles as a complete, all-in-one seasoning. You'll notice that most of my wet seasoning blends include green onions, garlic, hot peppers, and salt. The other ingredients, such as vegetables, herbs, and spices, vary from island to island.

Uncooked sauces, such as pickle, are used to enhance the flavor of Caribbean root vegetables. They're mostly found in French Caribbean cooking. An example is Sauce Chien (page 28), which is popular on the islands of Guadeloupe and Martinique. It accompanies most meals and works well on vegetables and starches.

Chutney is a staple sauce that is made in countries with high Indo-Caribbean populations, like Guyana and Trinidad and Tobago. Chutneys are made from locally grown produce such as mangoes, cucumbers, and coconuts. Chutneys range from sweet to sour, and some are savory and spicy.

Gravies and sauces are used widely on rice and other starchy dishes to provide flavor. These sauces are usually started by sautéing onions, tomatoes, and bell peppers. Gravies are usually not very thick like in the United States but are thin to medium thick in consistency, and are sometimes colored with browning, or some may have a tomato base.

The reason condiments are the first recipes in the book is that many of these condiments are used in the recipes throughout the book, so you'll want to make them first. I suggest making the Bajan Seasoning (page 19), Caribbean Caramel (page 25), and Bajan Pepper Sauce (page 23) first, as these are called for in many recipes.

Bajan Seasoning

MAKES 1 CUP (250 ML)

Bajan is the local word meaning "from Barbados," and this seasoning blend is in every kitchen pantry on the island. It doesn't really have a fixed recipe, so make it following this recipe the first time, then you can just use the recipe as a guideline and adjust it to suit your tastes or what you have on hand. It will turn out fine. Bajan Seasoning is great for flavoring tofu or seitan. You can also add it to soups and stews.

25 to 30 green onions

1 onion

3 to 5 garlic cloves

**1 to 2 Scotch bonnet or habanero peppers
(seeded if you prefer less spicy)**

Juice of 2 limes or Key limes

Handful of fresh thyme sprigs

Handful of fresh marjoram sprigs

2 tablespoons coarsely chopped parsley

1½ to 2 teaspoons salt

1 tablespoon black pepper

1 tablespoon mild paprika

1 teaspoon Madras curry powder

1 teaspoon ground cloves

⅓ cup (75 ml) distilled white vinegar

Coarsely chop green onions, onions, garlic, and Scotch bonnets by hand. Then put this mixture in a food processor and pulse until more finely chopped (see photo insert, page 2). Add the lime juice, thyme, marjoram, and parsley and pulse a few more times. Add the salt, black pepper, paprika, curry powder, cloves, and vinegar and process until medium smooth. There should still be some texture left in the seasoning.

Transfer to a clean jar, seal, and refrigerate. This seasoning blend will keep for as long as 1 year in the fridge.

Jamaican Jerk Seasoning

MAKES 1 CUP (250 ML)

This can be made as spicy or as mild as you want it. Although there are many recipes circulating for jerk seasoning, I wanted to design one especially for the recipes in this book. It delivers a lot of flavor but not too much heat. If you're very adventurous, use up to four Scotch bonnets with the seeds for a real kick. Like Bajan Seasoning (page 19), it has no fixed recipe, so use this version as a guide and feel free to improvise.

1 thick 3½ x 1-inch (9 x 2.5 cm) piece of fresh ginger

25 to 30 green onions

1 or 2 Scotch bonnet or habanero peppers
   (seeded if you prefer less spicy)

5 garlic cloves

Small bunch of fresh thyme

½ cup (125 ml) canola oil or another neutral-flavored oil

½ cup (125 ml) soy sauce

½ cup (125 ml) tomato sauce, preferably Spanish-style

⅓ cup (75 ml) fresh orange juice

⅓ cup (75 ml) distilled white vinegar

3 tablespoons fresh lime juice

3 tablespoons brown sugar

1½ tablespoons salt

1½ tablespoons ground cloves

1½ tablespoons ground allspice

1½ teaspoons ground nutmeg

¼ to ½ teaspoon ground cinnamon or cassia

Put the ginger, green onions, Scotch bonnets, garlic, and thyme in a food processor and process for 30 seconds. Add the oil, soy sauce, tomato sauce, orange juice, vinegar, lime juice, brown sugar, salt, cloves, allspice, nutmeg, and cinnamon and process until medium smooth.

Transfer to a clean jar, seal, and refrigerate. This seasoning blend will keep for as long as 1 year in the fridge.

 **ISLAND TIP**

What separates jerk seasoning from the Trinidadian Green Seasoning (page 22) and Bajan Seasoning (page 19) is the color, the cloves, and the allspice. In some recipes, dark rum is heated and added to the seasoning blend. Jerk seasoning is traditionally made with a mortar and pestle, including the crushing of the allspice. For the best flavor, use a Spanish-style tomato sauce. I like Goya brand. Spanish-style tomato sauce is slightly more acidic than regular tomato sauce, and also contains different spices. The color of jerk seasoning ranges from a rich reddish brown to almost dark brown. Jerk seasoning can be cured outside in the sun after bottling. To cure, place seasoning in a clear sterile jar, seal, and leave outside in the sun for three days.

Trinidadian Green Seasoning

You can use this condiment as a substitute for Bajan Seasoning (page 19) if you like, or if you don't have all of the ingredients for Bajan Seasoning. It won't keep for as long as the Bajan Seasoning or Jamaican Jerk Seasoning (page 20) because it doesn't contain spices that can help prevent microbial growth.

> 1 bunch of cilantro
> 20 green onions
> 1 onion, coarsely chopped
> 4 garlic cloves, coarsely chopped
> 1 Scotch bonnet or habanero pepper (seeded if you prefer less spicy)
> 3 mild chiles, such as Hungarian wax peppers
> ½ cup chopped parsley
> 3 tablespoons chopped rosemary
> ½ cup (125 ml) olive oil or canola oil
> 1 tablespoon salt

Put all of the ingredients in a food processor and process until smooth.

Transfer to clean jar, seal, and refrigerate. This seasoning blend will keep for as long as 1 month in the fridge.

 **ISLAND TIP**

You can omit the oil from this recipe if you want a more vibrant color and are using the entire amount right away to season a large amount of protein.

Bajan Pepper Sauce

This style of pepper sauce is what I grew up eating in Barbados, and this recipe is my personal go-to pepper sauce. The original recipe uses fresh turmeric, but that can be hard to come by. If you can't find it, you can substitute ground turmeric. Red Scotch bonnet peppers give this sauce its characteristic orange color with red flecks. Pepper sauce is something that some people can handle and others cannot. Start with just a bit and increase the amount gradually until you learn your limit. Because of its flavor and heat, pepper sauce used to be called a meal saver; if people found a dish unappetizing, they would add a bit of pepper sauce to make it more edible. Pepper sauce is used in sandwiches as well as in most soups and stews in Barbados, and it's almost always offered on the table at local restaurants. In a pinch, you can use Tabasco or another hot sauce in its place, but try to make this sauce. It will give your recipes authentic Caribbean flavor.

½ cup (125 ml) finely grated fresh turmeric,
   or 1 tablespoon ground turmeric

3 Scotch bonnet or habanero peppers (seeded if you prefer less spicy)

1 onion, coarsely chopped

2 large garlic cloves, coarsely chopped

1½ teaspoons salt

1 teaspoon brown sugar

⅓ cup American-style prepared mustard

2 tablespoons distilled white vinegar

Put all of the ingredients in a food processor and process until smooth.

Transfer to a clean jar, seal, and refrigerate. This pepper sauce will keep for as long as 1 year in the fridge.

☀ ISLAND TIP

Pepper sauce varies from island to island depending on the tastes of each island's inhabitants. Some use cucumber and green papaya for a base or incorporate sweet fruit. The pepper sauce may thicken a bit in the fridge. If that happens, just add a little vinegar or water and shake it up. If you haven't made this Bajan Pepper Sauce and need to use it in a recipe, you can approximate it by mixing about two parts commercial pepper sauce with one part American-style mustard.

Caribbean Caramel

This Caribbean Caramel is my version of browning, a natural food coloring used throughout the Caribbean to color dishes dark brown. Why would anyone want to color something dark brown? Why not? I use it to darken my lentil stews and puddings, and also in rice dishes such as Barbadian Pelau (page 104), where a brown color is typical for the dish. Browning is also used to darken chocolate cakes and gingerbread. It's available commercially, usually labeled "browning" or "coloring." You can use this recipe to make it at home, but be forewarned: Your smoke detector may go off due to the burning of the sugar. Also note that this recipe isn't something that you should taste; it's just a natural food coloring.

> 2 cups (400 g) brown sugar
> 1 tablespoon water
> ¾ cup (188 ml) cold water
> 2 tablespoons hot water

Put the sugar and the 1 tablespoon of water in a heavy skillet and spread out the sugar. Cook over medium heat for about 5 to 7 minutes, until the sugar goes from light brown to dark brown. Immediately add the ¾ cup cold water and cook, stirring constantly, for about five to seven minutes, or until the mixture gets thick and dark brown. Turn off the heat and stir in the hot water.

Cool to room temperature, then store in a glass bottle or jar with a lid. Store at room temperature. This should keep up to 6 months

☀ ISLAND TIP

 *A little goes* a long way. Be sure not to use too much, as it can give foods a bitter flavor.

Caribbean Pickle

MAKES 1 CUP (250 ML); SERVES 4

In the Caribbean, pickle is a cold, salty, acidic sauce that's ordinarily added to meat and vegetables. It's easy to make. Just grate everything, and in a few minutes you're done. My favorite food to use as a base for pickle is green bananas because they suck up all the flavor; my second favorite is breadfruit. Feel free to put this pickle on any root vegetables.

1 medium-large cucumber, peeled and grated or minced
1 onion, grated
Juice of 1 lime (if your lime is not juicy you will need 2)
1 Scotch bonnet or habanero pepper, minced
2 tablespoons finely chopped parsley or parsley leaves
1½ teaspoons salt
½ teaspoon minced fresh thyme, optional
1 teaspoon minced fresh dill, optional
½ teaspoon minced marjoram, optional
¼ cup water (62 ml)

Combine all of the ingredients in the order listed. Set aside at room temperature for 30 minutes and then place in the refrigerator. This pickle must be consumed within 5 hours of preparation because the taste will change drastically after this time due to the lime juice in the dish.

Taste and adjust for lime and salt. When you taste this pickle, you will first taste the lime, then the salt, then the onion, then the parsley, and then the hot pepper.

☀ ISLAND TIP

To make pickle the traditional way, you must chip the onion and cucumber with a knife. Chipping results in smaller, finer pieces than traditional dicing. To chip a cucumber or an onion, cut off the top to form a new, flat top. Make close, shallow cuts across the top, first horizontally and then vertically, forming a grid of tiny cubes. Then turn the onion or cucumber sideways and slice the cubes off into a bowl. This will leave a new flat top, so continue chipping until you've done the whole thing. Alternatively, you can mince the cucumbers and onion finely. Chipping creates a more textured finished product for a better presentation.

Breadfruit is sold canned in brine, but in summer you may be able to find it fresh at Asian or Latin American markets. If using canned breadfruit, heat it briefly before adding the other ingredients, and reduce the amount of salt to ¼ teaspoon.

Pickle has no recipe per se. Adjust the seasoning to suit your own tastes, using this recipe as a guide.

Sauce Chien

If you aren't familiar with the French West Indies, this refers to Guadeloupe, Martinique, Saint Martin, and Saint Barts. These islands are still governed by France, and the inhabitants speak French exclusively except on Saint Martin, where they are bilingual and even trilingual. Most of the food on these islands is inspired by French cuisine. *Sauce chien* translated from French Creole means "dogfish sauce" in English. This sauce is most often used as a condiment on a fish consumed in the French West Indies called dogfish. If you have a mortar and pestle, you can use it for this recipe; try to avoid using a food processor as it will over-process all of the ingredients and the finished product will be too smooth and not like the traditional sauce.

4 green onions (white part only), minced
½ onion, minced
3 garlic cloves, minced
½ to 1 teaspoon minced Scotch bonnet or habanero pepper
1 tablespoon minced parsley
¼ cup (62 ml) canola oil or another neutral-flavored oil
1½ tablespoons fresh lime juice
1 teaspoon distilled white vinegar
¼ cup (62 ml) hot water
½ teaspoon granulated sugar
½ teaspoon salt
¼ teaspoon black pepper

Combine the green onions, onion, garlic, Scotch bonnet, and parsley in a small bowl.

Separately, mix the oil, lime juice, and vinegar together, then whisk in the hot water until emulsified. Stir in the sugar, salt, and black pepper. Pour the mixture over the chopped vegetables and mix well.

Let the sauce sit at room temperature for 1 hour before serving to enhance the flavor. Store any leftovers in a clean jar in the refrigerator. This sauce will keep for as long as 3 days in the fridge.

ISLAND TIP

Try this sauce on cooked vegetables, fries and other potato dishes, rice dishes, and even Island Burgers (page 114). Vendors sell dehydrated dogfish sauce in the markets in Guadeloupe. You just reconstitute it with a little water, add some salt and a little oil, and it's ready.

Green Mango Chutney

Trinidad and Tobago has a high Indo-Caribbean population, so it is no wonder that their recipes have a strong Indian influence. Trinidad is known for its amazing chutneys. A while back, I developed this recipe because I couldn't wait for my mangoes to ripen. Little did I know that there was such a thing as green mango chutney in Trinidad and Tobago. Don't confuse this with Western mango chutney, which is sweet; this condiment is savory with a peppery kick. This is excellent on Trinidadian Doubles (page 112).

4 medium or 1 large green, unripe mangoes, peeled and finely grated

3 garlic cloves, pressed

1 tablespoon olive oil

⅛ teaspoon minced Scotch bonnet or habanero pepper, or a pinch of cayenne pepper

1 teaspoon finely chopped parsley

¼ teaspoon black pepper

½ teaspoon brown sugar

½ teaspoon salt, or to taste

Mix all of the ingredients together. Transfer to a jar, seal, and refrigerate. This chutney will keep for as long as 4 days in the fridge.

Trinidadian Coconut Chutney

The coconut for this chutney is fire-roasted on a stove top before being grated. The result is a smoky condiment that is addictive and works well on Caribbean rice dishes. You need fairly large pieces of coconut so that you can easily hold them over the flame with tongs. I love this chutney with Barbadian Pelau (page 104), or on any rice dish.

> **Flesh of ½ coconut, in large pieces**
> **3 tablespoons chopped cilantro**
> **1 Scotch bonnet or habanero pepper**
> **5 large garlic cloves**
> **1½ cups (375 ml) water**
> **1 teaspoon fresh lime juice**
> **1¼ teaspoons salt**

Using tongs, roast the coconut over an open flame until black and charred. Cool the coconut.

Once the coconut is cool enough to handle, scrape off a bit the charred outer layer. Finely grate the coconut, then put it in a food processor. Add the cilantro, Scotch bonnet, garlic, water, lime juice, and salt and process until fairly smooth.

Transfer the chutney to a clean jar, seal, and refrigerate. It will keep for as long as 2 weeks in the fridge.

 ISLAND TIP

The coconut absorbs a lot of water, so if you store the chutney for a while, you may need to add a little water. You can leave on the thin brown skin on the coconut for this recipe. It won't affect the taste or the texture.

Cucumber Chutney

This chutney, which is similar to an uncooked Caribbean pickle, is sometimes served on Trinidadian Doubles (page 112) to add a crunchy, spicy kick.

1 cucumber, with skin, finely grated

1 tablespoon grated onion

½ teaspoon minced Scotch bonnet pepper

1 teaspoon fresh lime juice

½ teaspoon salt

½ teaspoon ground cumin

Put all of the ingredients in a small bowl and stir until well combined. Let the chutney stand for 20 minutes. This gives some time for the cucumber to release its juices, making the chutney saucier.

Pineapple Barbecue Sauce

MAKES 2 CUPS (500 ML)

There are many great home cooks in the Caribbean who create their own barbecue sauce. Some of them sell their fare on the streets, and each of these vendors is known for the type of barbecue sauce they make. Many Caribbean-style barbecue sauces call for fruit flavors, like pineapple and passion fruit. In this recipe, I've used pineapple as my fruit. You can quickly whip up pineapple barbecue sauce by blending up some pineapple and pineapple juice and adding them to a standard barbecue sauce, but this is a cookbook, so I had to give you a recipe for making it from scratch so you could get your money's worth.

7 garlic cloves

½ onion, chopped

2 green onions, chopped

2 tomatoes, chopped

1 teaspoon minced ginger

4 rings of canned pineapple

⅓ cup (75 ml) pineapple juice
(from the canned pineapple if it's packed in its own juice)

½ cup (125 ml) ketchup

¼ cup (62 ml) apple cider vinegar

2 tablespoons soy sauce

1½ tablespoons Jamaican Jerk Seasoning (page 20)
or Bajan Seasoning (page 19)

1 tablespoon unsulfured blackstrap molasses

1 tablespoon Angostura bitters

1 tablespoon liquid smoke, or to taste

1 tablespoon rum, optional

2 teaspoons American-style prepared mustard

1 teaspoon Caribbean Caramel (page 25) or browning

1 teaspoon Bajan Pepper Sauce (page 23)

¾ cup (150 g) brown sugar

2 tablespoons salt

1 teaspoon black pepper

1 teaspoon chili powder, optional

½ teaspoon ground allspice

½ teaspoon ground cloves

1 cup (250 ml) water

1½ tablespoons cornstarch

1 teaspoon Bajan Seasoning (page 19)

Put 5 of the garlic cloves in a blender or food processor. Add the onions, tomatoes, ginger, pineapple, pineapple juice, ketchup, vinegar, soy sauce, jerk seasoning, molasses, bitters, liquid smoke, optional rum, mustard, Caribbean Caramel, pepper sauce, sugar, salt, pepper, optional chili powder, allspice, and ground cloves. Process until very smooth.

Transfer the mixture to a saucepan and cook over low heat for 25 minutes, stirring occasionally, and adding half the water. In a separate bowl, stir the cornstarch into the remaining water. Add the cornstarch mixture to the saucepan, whisking until no lumps remain, and cook for 5 more minutes. Remove from the heat and let cool for 20 minutes to make it safe for blending.

Transfer the sauce back to the food processor or blender and add the remaining 2 garlic cloves and the Bajan seasoning. Process until smooth. Taste and adjust the seasonings, adding more liquid smoke if you like. Depending on how concentrated the liquid smoke is, you might add as much as 5 more tablespoons.

Transfer to a clean jar, seal, and refrigerate. This sauce will keep for as long as 6 months in the fridge.

ISLAND TIP

This sauce is a great dip for Spicy Baked Sweet Potato Wedges (page 148), or just as a replacement for regular barbecue sauce. If you like, spice it up by adding 2 Scotch bonnet peppers, including their seeds.

Onion Gravy

This brown, flavorful gravy is used in some parts of the Caribbean by people who don't eat meat. It's great on potatoes and other root vegetables and also on plain rice dishes. You can omit the Caribbean Caramel if you don't care about the brown color.

1 tablespoon vegan margarine or olive oil

1 medium-large onion, thinly sliced

1 tomato, thinly sliced

2 garlic cloves, pressed

1 teaspoon fresh marjoram minced, or a scant ½ teaspoon dried

1 teaspoon fresh thyme minced, or ¼ teaspoon dried

1 teaspoon onion powder

1 teaspoon adobo seasoning

¼ teaspoon mild paprika

1 cup (250 ml) water

2 tablespoons ketchup

1 teaspoon soy sauce

¼ teaspoon Caribbean Caramel (page 25) or browning

¼ teaspoon cornstarch

½ teaspoon American-style mustard

Heat the margarine in a skillet over medium heat. Add the onion, tomato, and garlic and sauté for about 3 to 5 minutes, until the onion is slightly tender. Add the marjoram, thyme, onion powder, adobo seasoning, and paprika, then stir in the water. Cook for another 5 minutes, then stir in ketchup, soy sauce, Caribbean Caramel, cornstarch mixed with 1 tablespoon of water, and mustard. Simmer, stirring occasionally for about 15 minutes, until the sauce starts to get slightly thick. Serve hot.

Creole Sauce

If there is a multipurpose gravy in the Caribbean, it's this sauce. It's similar to Onion Gravy (page 35), but the tomato paste gives it a bright orange color. It's terrific on Cou-Cou (page 122).

6 tablespoons (86 g) vegan margarine
6 tomatoes, thinly sliced
2 onions, thinly sliced
4 garlic cloves, chopped
1 teaspoon black pepper
1 teaspoon mild paprika
1 teaspoon Madras curry powder
2 cups (500 ml) water
2 teaspoons tomato paste
1½ to 2 teaspoons salt, or to taste
2 teaspoons onion powder
1 teaspoon minced parsley
1 to 2 teaspoons Bajan Pepper Sauce (page 23)

Heat the margarine in a large saucepan over low heat. Add the tomatoes and onions and sauté until the tomatoes begin to release their juice and the onions start to become translucent. Add the garlic, raise the heat to medium, and cook for 3 minutes. Stir in the pepper, paprika, and curry powder, then stir in the water and tomato paste. Cook for 5 minutes, stirring occasionally. Stir in the salt, onion powder, parsley, and pepper sauce. Serve hot.

 ISLAND TIP

The pepper sauce rounds out the flavor of this sauce. If you don't have any Bajan Pepper Sauce on hand, you can use 1 teaspoon commercial pepper sauce; just mix in ½ teaspoon of American-style mustard for more authentic flavor.

Curry Sauce

I started making this version of curry sauce when I was in secondary school. It doesn't contain either coconut milk or cream, so isn't as rich as other recipes for curry sauce. It's great served on hot white rice, and a slab of Tofish (page 120) alongside. Because cornmeal is used to thicken this sauce, it will solidify at room temperature. So if you are reheating it, you will probably need to add as much as ¼ cup water.

2 tablespoons vegan margarine

½ onion, minced

1 small bay leaf

1 to 2 tablespoons minced celery

1 tablespoon Madras curry powder

1 tablespoon fine cornmeal or corn flour

⅓ cup (75 ml) water

½ teaspoon salt

¼ teaspoon ground ginger

1½ teaspoons fresh lime juice

Heat the margarine in a small saucepan over medium heat. Add the onion, bay leaf, and celery, turn the heat down to medium-low, and sauté for about 5 minutes, until the onion is translucent. Add the curry powder, cornmeal, and water and whisk briskly. Stir in the salt and ginger, raise the heat to medium, and cook for 4 minutes, stirring occasionally, until the sauce is slightly thick. Remove from the heat and stir in the lime juice.

BREAKFAST
DISHES

WE ALL KNOW that breakfast is the most important meal of the day, yet we still sometimes skip it. During colonial times, breakfast was considered the most important meal of the day because workers in the sugarcane fields needed all the energy they could get. Caribbean breakfast dishes were molded to fit the industrial period of sugarcane production: high-energy dishes that contained corn, barley, and wheat. Field workers packed items like porridge or johnny-cakes (see page 41) and ate them with tea or Mauby (page 213) and sugar-water. Breakfast was usually eaten at 10 AM, since this was when field workers got a break. Before these workers left home, they would have bush tea, made from herbs and plants growing in their gardens. This tea would sustain them until 10 AM. Even now, many people in the Caribbean eat breakfast later than elsewhere. They call this breakfast "break," and it is basically brunch.

In the early days, most breakfast dishes were savory, which may be due to the influence of British culture. If an island changed hands, the cuisine, including breakfast dishes, often evolved to reflect the change. Patties—pastries stuffed with various savory fillings—were often eaten for breakfast. You'll find recipes for patties in the chapter on Entrées (page 97).

Today, breakfast in the Caribbean has become very Americanized, with foods like ready-made pancake mixes and sausages widely available. However, many people still enjoy the traditional breakfast dishes that shaped our food culture.

Saint Lucian Bakes

MAKES THREE 3-INCH (8 CM) BAKES

My grandmother moved to Barbados from Saint Lucia in the 1950s and brought many traditions with her, including these bakes, which are a Caribbean version of English muffins. They're similar to Barbadian Muffins (page 44) but savory. Bakes can be used as bread, and you can stuff anything inside. Tasty fillings include vegan cheese, jam, sliced Everyday Vegan "Ham" (page 100), or simply margarine. They can be also enjoyed plain, with a cup of tea. On some islands, like Saint Martin in the French West Indies, bakes are sold as a street food called johnnycakes.

> 1¼ cups (156 g) unbleached all-purpose flour
> ½ teaspoon salt
> 1 teaspoon baking powder
> ⅓ cup (75 ml) ice-cold water
> Canola oil

Sift the flour, then stir in the salt and baking powder in a large bowl. Slowly add the cold water, and bring the dough together with your hands. Form the dough into a ball and knead in the bowl for about 5 minutes, until it starts to get elastic. If the dough appears overly dry, add another tablespoon or two of water. Let the dough rest for 5 minutes.

Divide the dough into 3 equal pieces. Shape each into a ball, then flatten into a disk about 1 inch (2.5 cm) thick. To form the dough, continually fold the outer edges of the disk into the center as if you were going to make a hole in the center. Let bakes relax for 15 minutes before frying; this will help them plump up and have a softer texture.

Heat about ¾ inch (2 cm) of vegetable oil in a large, heavy skillet over medium-high heat. To test if the oil is hot enough to add the bakes, sprinkle a little flour in the oil; it is ready when there is a strong sizzle. Carefully add the bakes to the oil and cook for 45 seconds to form a crust on the outside, then lower the heat to medium-low and allow the bakes to cook slowly for about 5 to 7 minutes, until browned on one side. Turn the bakes, and raise the heat to medium-high briefly, to form a crust. (For a softer crust, don't increase the heat.) Fry for about 15 minutes total, turning about twice more. Cut into the center of one bake to ensure that the inside is well cooked.

Drain on paper towels and serve warm.

ISLAND TIP

In the Caribbean, we call these quick breads *bakes* even though they aren't baked. They may also be called johnnycakes or johnny bakes. You can make a version of this recipe using whole wheat flour—just increase the amount of baking powder to 1½ teaspoons.

Cornmeal Bakes

These Bajan Cornmeal Bakes are quite different from the Saint Lucian Bakes (page 41). The batter is similar to pancake batter but a little firmer, and they're cooked differently than pancakes. They're fried in big clumps rather than flat, and with a little more oil than typically used for pancakes. The result is crispy on the outside and soft and fluffy on the inside. Although they are considered an old-fashioned food, there is nothing old-fashioned about the taste. They are perfect for brunch as a change from pancakes and waffles. Serve them on their own, or with jam.

¾ cup (95 g) unbleached all-purpose flour

½ cup (60 g) fine cornmeal or corn flour

¼ cup (30 g) millet flour or another ¼ cup fine cornmeal or corn flour

2 tablespoons light brown sugar

2 teaspoons baking powder

½ teaspoon salt

1 teaspoon ground cinnamon or cassia

¼ teaspoon ground nutmeg

½ teaspoon vanilla essence or ¼ teaspoon vanilla extract

1 cup (250 ml) nondairy milk

Canola oil

Stir the flour, cornmeal, millet flour, sugar, baking powder, salt, cinnamon, and nutmeg together. Stir the vanilla into the nondairy milk. Add the milk to the flour mixture and mix lightly, until just combined.

Heat about ¾ inch (2 cm) of oil in a large, heavy skillet over medium heat. Test the oil by dropping a little bit of batter into the oil; the oil is ready when the batter sizzles vigorously. (Do not forget to remove this small piece of batter from the oil.) Carefully spoon the batter into the oil, using about 2 heaping tablespoons of batter for each bake. Turn the heat down to medium-low and fry the bakes for about 5 minutes, turning frequently to cook both sides evenly. The bakes are ready when they are golden brown with a crispy exterior.

Drain on paper towels. Serve warm.

Barbadian Muffins

Barbadians have a sweet tooth. This is their take on the English muffin. A nice vegan cheddar would be a good accompaniment.

¼ teaspoon apple cider vinegar

½ cup plus 1 tablespoon (140 ml) nondairy milk

1½ cups (375 ml) unbleached all-purpose flour

2 tablespoons light brown sugar

1 tablespoon baking powder

1 teaspoon salt

½ teaspoon ground cinnamon or cassia

½ teaspoon ground nutmeg

2 tablespoons vegetable shortening

⅔ cup (158 ml) canola oil

Stir the vinegar into the ½ cup nondairy milk. Separately, mix the flour, sugar, baking powder, salt, cinnamon, and nutmeg together in a bowl. Add the shortening and rub it in to the flour with your fingertips or a pastry blender. Slowly pour in the milk and stir until the dough comes together.

Knead dough in the bowl for 4 minutes, until the dough is mixed well and slightly elastic. Let the dough relax for 15 minutes.

Cut the dough into 6 equal pieces and pat each into a disk about ½ inch (1.3 cm) thick.

Heat the oil in a large skillet over medium-high heat. Add the dough pieces and cook for 20 seconds on one side. Turn them immediately and cook for 30 seconds. Turn the heat down to low and cook the muffins for 10 minutes, turning every 2 minutes. The finished muffins should be light and crispy with a golden brown color.

Drain the muffins on paper towels and serve warm.

Sweet Potato Drop Biscuits

This savory and sweet biscuit is not a traditional Caribbean recipe, but the flavor profile is typical of island cuisine, and it is a good way to use orange-fleshed sweet potatoes. In the Caribbean, biscuits are usually obtained from fast-food outlets that offer typical American fare. I have included these because I think they are a good substitute for buttermilk biscuits. These biscuits don't fit into the category of savory or sweet—that is why they are good with either savory scrambles or jam.

7 ounces (200 g) orange-fleshed sweet potatoes, peeled and chopped
2 cups (250 g) unbleached all-purpose flour
1 teaspoon salt
½ teaspoon baking soda
½ teaspoon ground cinnamon
⅛ teaspoon ground cloves
½ cup (113 g) cold vegan margarine
¼ cup (50 g) brown sugar
2 teaspoons baking powder
¾ cup (188 ml) nondairy milk

Cook the sweet potatoes in boiling salted water for about 20 minutes, until just tender. Preheat the oven to 400°F (200°C). Lightly grease a baking sheet.

Stir the flour, salt, baking soda, cinnamon, and cloves together. Add the margarine and rub it into the flour with your fingertips or a pastry blender until the mixture has the texture of coarse bread crumbs. Add the brown sugar, baking powder, and nondairy milk and mix lightly, until just combined.

Drop 2 heaping tablespoons of the batter onto the prepared baking sheet for each biscuit, leaving at least 1½ inches (4 cm) between them. Bake for about 20 minutes, until golden brown. Serve warm.

Herbed Sada Roti

In Trinidad and Tobago, Guyana, and many other countries with a strong Indian influence, Sada Roti is served for breakfast with Eggplant Choka (page 69). If you compare the ingredients, you will see that, other than the herbs and garlic, this recipe has the almost the same ingredients as Saint Lucian Bakes. However, the end result is totally different. Sada Roti is a flatbread that puffs up at the sides when cooked. Traditional sada roti is plain, without the herbs and garlic. You can leave them out if you like. If you do not have a tawa (see page 12), you can use a large frying pan or griddle to cook up your rotis.

> **2 cups (250 g) unbleached all-purpose flour**
> **2 teaspoons baking powder**
> **½ teaspoon salt**
> **1 cup (250 ml) water, or more as needed**
> **2 teaspoons chopped herbs, optional**
> **1 garlic clove, minced, optional**
> **Canola oil or another neutral-flavored oil**

Put the flour, baking powder, salt, water, and optional herbs and garlic in a bowl and stir until the dough comes together. Knead the dough in the bowl for about 4 minutes, until smooth. If the dough is too dry, add 1 or 2 more teaspoons of water. If too wet, add 1 or 2 tablespoons of flour.

Put the dough in a lightly oiled bowl in a warm, draft-free place, cover, and let rise for about 1½ hours, until it has risen slightly and has taken on softer texture.

Divide the dough into 4 equal pieces and form them into balls. At this stage, the dough should be very smooth. Return the balls to the oiled bowl, cover, and let rise for 2 hours.

Working on a lightly floured surface, roll the roti out to a thickness of ¼ inch (6 mm). Heat a tawa, griddle, or large, heavy skillet over medium heat. Lightly oil the tawa and place the first roti on the tawa. Cook for 4 to 5 minutes, turning periodically, until both sides start to develop brown spots. The roti should be filled with air, especially at the edges. Oil the pan before cooking the next roti. Cut the roti into pieces and serve warm.

ISLAND TIP

Sada roti dough can be left to rest for up to 5 hours in a warm place after dividing it into balls. These rotis work well as an appetizer when served with Eggplant Choka (page 69) for lunch or dinner.

Salt Bread

Every island has their go-to bread for sandwiches. The Jamaicans have coco bread (which, as it happens, contains neither coconut nor cacao), the Trinidadians have hops bread, and Bajans have salt bread. I wish I could share all of the recipes for island rolls, but since I had to choose one, I went with the salt bread, since its recipe can be hard to come by. Salt bread recipes have always been a closely guarded secret in Barbados. The name *salt bread* doesn't mean that this bread is particularly salty, just that it is savory bread. It has a soft, floury crust, and when you bite into it, you get a flour moustache and a pillowy-soft interior. Old-fashioned salt breads are made with white flour and a coconut palm leaf on top of each bread so that when the bread rises, it bursts, giving it a rustic appearance. You can create a similar appearance by slitting the top and sides with a knife.

One ¼-ounce package (2½ teaspoons / 7 g) active dry yeast

2 teaspoons brown sugar

1 cup (250 ml) warm water (110°F to 115°F / 43°C to 46°C), or more as needed

4 cups (500 g) unbleached all-purpose flour

1½ teaspoons salt

2 tablespoons plus 1 teaspoon vegan margarine, melted

Coconut palm pieces, optional

Stir the yeast and sugar into the water and let stand for about 15 minutes, until the top is foamy. (If the yeast doesn't foam, it's dead or the water was too hot or too cool. You need to start over with fresh yeast.)

Put the flour and salt in a bowl and stir to combine. Add the yeast mixture and the melted margarine and stir until the dough comes together.

Knead the dough in the bowl for 7 minutes, until it is very soft and slightly tacky.

Put the dough in a lightly oiled bowl in a warm, draft-free place, cover, and let rise until doubled in size. This could take anywhere from 1½ hours in a tropical climate to 3 hours in a temperate climate or longer in a cold climate.

Grease a baking sheet. Punch down the dough and divide it into 6 pieces. The dough should be very smooth and easy to work with. Form each piece into a pear shape and place the pieces on the prepared baking sheet. Cut two slits into the top of the bread or place optional coconut palm pieces at the top. Gently brush the bread with water. Put the baking sheet in a warm, draft-free place, cover, and let the dough rise for 1 to 2½ hours, until the formed breads have doubled in size.

Preheat the oven to 400°F (200°C).

Re-brush the breads with some water and bake them for 15 to 20 minutes, until golden brown. Let cool for 30 minutes before serving.

 **ISLAND TIP**

Brushing the bread with water is responsible for softening the crust at the end; this is a tip I received from a Barbadian baker.

When temperatures are cool, it can take a long time for the bread to rise. Here's a way to create an ideal rising environment for any yeast dough: Turn on the oven for a few minutes and then turn it off. You will have created a perfect warm environment in which the bread can rise, simulating a warmer island climate.

Any sandwich made with salt bread is called a cutter. If you have cheese in your salt bread, it's called a cheese cutter. Don't try to speak too correctly when saying it: it's pronounced "cuttah."

Coconut Orange Pancakes

Pancakes became popular in the Caribbean in the late 1980s. Many Caribbean nationals had emigrated to the United States and Canada, and when they returned, they made pancakes in the morning for their families. I loved pancakes, but after I went vegan I gave up hope of eating them because I thought I would never be able to achieve a fluffy, soft pancake without eggs. But eventually I did, and today I'm a happy vegan pancake lover. Try these pancakes for your next brunch. The candied coconut is optional, but I highly recommend it.

CANDIED SPICED COCONUT

¼ cup (25 g) coconut or unsweetened dried coconut

¼ cup (62 ml) fresh orange juice

3 tablespoons (45 ml) water

1 tablespoon brown sugar

⅛ teaspoon ground nutmeg

Pinch of ground cinnamon

PANCAKES

1 teaspoon apple cider vinegar

1¼ cups (313 ml) nondairy milk

¾ cup (94 g) unbleached all-purpose flour

½ cup (60 g) whole wheat flour

2 teaspoons baking powder

½ teaspoon baking soda

2 tablespoons light brown sugar or granulated sugar

½ cup (50 g) finely grated fresh coconut

1½ teaspoons almond essence, or ¾ teaspoon almond extract

½ teaspoon orange zest

½ cup (125 ml) fresh orange juice

½ teaspoon salt

Vegan margarine

Orange sections, optional

To make the candied coconut, combine all of the ingredients in a small saucepan over low heat. Cook, stirring occasionally, for about 15 minutes, until the liquid is reduced by about half. If you want a drier coconut mixture, cook for an additional 10 minutes, until the coconut is cooked.

To make the pancakes, stir the vinegar into the nondairy milk. Separately, stir the flours, baking powder, baking soda, and sugar together. Add the coconut, almond essence, and orange zest to the milk. Pour the milk mixture into the flour mixture and stir to incorporate. Stir in the orange juice and salt and mix well. Refrigerate for 20 minutes to help the batter thicken.

Heat a griddle or large, heavy skillet over medium-low heat. Once it's hot, put a little margarine in the pan. Spoon the batter into the pan, using a scant ¼ cup (62 ml) for each pancake. Cook the pancakes for about 3½ to 4 minutes on each side, until golden brown.

Decorate the pancakes with the candied coconut, orange sections, and chocolate ganache (see Island Tip) if desired.

ISLAND TIP

If you want denser pancakes, add ¼ cup (31 g) more flour of your choice. To make chocolate ganache, just melt some dark chocolate, then stir in a bit of nondairy milk—but not too much. The ganache should be quite thick.

Banana Fritters

There are two ways to make banana fritters. Nationals of the French West Indies make a batter, dip pieces of rum-soaked banana into it, and fry them. In the English-speaking Caribbean, we usually blend mashed banana into a batter. If you are a banana lover, these doughnut-like fritters will fix your craving.

2 to 3 overripe bananas

1½ tablespoons brown sugar

1 teaspoon ground cinnamon

1 teaspoon ground nutmeg

1½ teaspoons vanilla essence, or ¾ teaspoon vanilla extract

1 teaspoon Angostura bitters

1¼ cups (156 g) unbleached all-purpose flour

1 teaspoon baking powder

1 teaspoon cornstarch

3 tablespoons nondairy milk

¼ teaspoon salt

¼ teaspoon baking soda

Canola oil

Granulated sugar

Put the bananas in a bowl and mash until very smooth. Stir in the brown sugar, cinnamon, nutmeg, essence, and bitters. Add the flour and baking powder and stir until well combined. Stir the cornstarch into the nondairy milk. Pour the milk into the batter, add the salt and baking soda, and mix well.

Heat about ¾ inch (2 cm) of oil in a large, heavy skillet over medium-high heat. Test if the oil is ready by spooning a little batter into the oil; it is ready when the batter sizzles vigorously and floats to the surface. (Do not forget to remove this small piece of batter from the oil.) Carefully spoon the batter into the oil, using about 1 heaping tablespoon for each fritter. Cook for 1 minute, then turn the heat down to medium, turn the fritters, and cook for 4 more minutes, turning periodically.

Drain on paper towels. Sprinkle with the granulated sugar and serve warm.

 **ISLAND TIP**

Reducing the flour by ¼ cup makes more concentrated banana fritters.

Pumpkin Fritters

In the Caribbean, calabaza squash is called pumpkin (or more specifically, West Indian pumpkin), so we call these pumpkin fritters. They are fried morsels of a batter made with grated calabaza squash, sugar, and spices. They are eaten for breakfast in the Caribbean, sprinkled with sugar. They actually taste like a pumpkin doughnut.

> 1 cup (250 ml) finely grated calabaza squash, pumpkin, or other winter squash
>
> 1 tablespoon nondairy milk
>
> 1 teaspoon vanilla extract
>
> ⅔ cup (85 g) unbleached all-purpose flour
>
> 2 tablespoons light brown sugar
>
> 1 teaspoon baking powder
>
> 1 teaspoon cornstarch
>
> ½ teaspoon ground nutmeg
>
> ½ teaspoon ground cinnamon or cassia
>
> ¼ teaspoon salt
>
> Canola oil
>
> Granulated sugar

Mix the calabaza squash, nondairy milk, vanilla, flour, sugar, baking powder, cornstarch, nutmeg, cinnamon, and salt together until well combined. The batter should be fairly soft but still stiff. Refrigerate for 20 minutes to help the batter thicken.

Heat about ¾ inch (2 cm) of oil in a large, heavy skillet over medium heat. Test if the oil is ready by spooning a little batter into the oil; it is ready when the batter sizzles vigorously and floats to the surface. (Do not forget to remove this small piece of batter from the oil.) Carefully spoon the batter into the oil, using about a heaping tablespoon batter for each fritter. Cook for 35 seconds, then turn the fritters over and cook for 30 seconds. Turn the heat down to low and cook the fritters, turning often, for about 5 minutes, until the fritters are golden brown.

Drain on paper towels. Sprinkle with granulated sugar and serve warm.

Hearts of Palm and Tofu Scramble

SERVES 4

Hearts of palm show up in recipes from the French West Indies and Spanish-speaking regions. They have a slightly acidic taste and are primarily available canned. The taste of the dish will be very different depending on which of the wet seasoning blends you use.

10 ounces (285 g) firm tofu, cut into 1¼-inch (3 cm) cubes

1 tablespoon Bajan Seasoning (page 19), Jamaican Jerk Seasoning (page 20), or Trinidadian Green Seasoning (page 22), or more to taste

2 tablespoons olive oil or coconut oil

7 to 14 ounces (200 to 400 g) hearts of palm, sliced

1 onion, finely chopped

2 green onions, finely chopped

1 tomato, coarsely chopped

1½ teaspoons chopped Scotch bonnet or habanero pepper

1 tablespoon parsley

1 teaspoon chopped fresh thyme, or ¼ teaspoon dried

1 teaspoon Madras curry powder

½ teaspoon black pepper

½ teaspoon ground cumin

1 tablespoon Bragg Liquid Aminos or soy sauce

1 teaspoon Angostura bitters

1 teaspoon vegan Worcestershire sauce

Salt

Toss the tofu with the Bajan Seasoning or whatever wet seasoning you like.

Heat the olive oil in a large skillet over medium heat. Add the coated tofu and cook for about 5 to 7 minutes, turning as needed to lightly brown all sides. Add the onions, green onions, tomato, Scotch bonnet, parsley, thyme, curry powder, black pepper, cumin, Bragg Liquid Aminos, bitters, and Worcestershire sauce. Turn the heat down to medium-low and sauté for 15 to 20 minutes, until all the vegetables are well cooked.

Season with salt to taste, and add more black pepper if you like. Serve warm.

Ackee Scramble

This recipe will have you talking about Jamaican ackee for a long time. Ackee is a fruit related to the lychee and longan. It is native to West Africa and was first brought to Jamaica in the 1700s. Ackee and salt fish is the national dish of Jamaica, but since we are vegan, let's forget the fish and add in other familiar flavors. Fresh ackee is not widely available outside the areas where it is grown, and unripe or improperly prepared ackee is poisonous. Since fresh ackee is not exported to the United States and Canada, look for canned ackee. Canned ackee is slightly inferior to fresh, but the laws in the U.S. make it difficult to import fresh ackee, so canned is the best option. When you open a can of ackee, drain it and wash off the brine before using it. Serve this scramble alongside Saint Lucian Bakes (page 41) or over white rice. Ackee is similar in color and texture to scrambled eggs.

2 tablespoons vegan margarine

½ cup (100 g) chopped smoky vegan sausage or Everyday Vegan "Ham" (page 100), coarsely chopped

½ teaspoon liquid smoke

½ onion, finely chopped

¼ red bell pepper, finely chopped

¼ green bell pepper, finely chopped

2 small tomatoes, chopped

1 green onion, minced

¼ teaspoon finely chopped Scotch bonnet or habanero pepper

One 19-ounce (540 ml) can Jamaican ackee, drained and gently rinsed

1 teaspoon chopped fresh thyme, or ¼ teaspoon dried

¼ teaspoon salt

¼ teaspoon black pepper

1 nori sheet, toasted and crumbled (see page 9), optional

Heat the margarine in a large skillet over medium-high heat. Add the vegan sausage and liquid smoke and cook for 2 minutes, until slightly browned. Add the onion, bell peppers, tomatoes, green onion, and Scotch bonnet. Turn down the heat to medium-low and sauté for 4 minutes, until the onions are translucent.

Turn the heat up to medium-high, add the ackee to the skillet, and gently stir it in. Cook, stirring gently from time to time, for 3 minutes, until a little sauce starts to develop in the skillet. Gently stir in the thyme, salt, black pepper, and optional nori. Turn the heat down to medium-low and cook for 4 minutes, stirring gently from time to time, until all the ingredients are cooked.

APPETIZERS

I HAVE BEEN fascinated with party food since childhood. One of my fondest childhood memories is admiring a party table, adorned with spicy sandwiches, grapefruit with cheese and sausage sticks, and hot fritters, all of which would disappear as soon as the host or hostess brought them out. Most of those appetizers have migrated to street food status, and most are spicy. These are not the type of appetizers that would be presented as the first course of a meal; they are the snacks that people would eat at a social gathering or if they felt hungry on the way to work. At parties, they are served buffet-style. The most popular appetizers are *accras*, a type of savory fritter offered on toothpicks with a sauce served alongside. Many Caribbean nationals also pack appetizers for big family picnics.

Eggplant and Seaweed Accras

Accras are a type of savory fritter, and in the Caribbean, they are also food that men often eat after work, accompanied by a cold beer. If you visit the French West Indies and the English-speaking Caribbean, you will see street vendors offering these fritters, with a long, snaking line of potential customers. Unfortunately, most of these fritters are not vegan. They are often made with fish, in which case they are known as fishcakes. Good news: I have developed a recipe, based on eggplant, which will trick even the most serious of fishcake eaters. Eggplant stands in for the fish, seaweed gives the fritters their characteristic flavor, and the Scotch bonnet gives it a spicy kick. Make these for your next dinner party just before guests arrive, or serve them for breakfast with Saint Lucian Bakes (page 41). Or you can put them in Salt Bread (page 48) to make a vegan "bread and two." (A traditional bread and two is two fishcakes in salt bread.)

1 eggplant, peeled and cut into short, thin strips

2½ teaspoons salt

1 tablespoon canola oil or another neutral-flavored oil, plus more for frying

3 nori sheets, toasted and crumbled (see page 9)

1 onion, finely chopped

3 to 4 green onions, minced

1 Scotch bonnet or habanero pepper, seeded and minced

2 teaspoons chopped fresh thyme

½ teaspoon black pepper

2 cups (250 g) unbleached all-purpose flour

1½ teaspoons baking powder

¾ to 1 cup (176 ml to 250 ml) water

Sprinkle the eggplant with 1½ teaspoons of the salt and let it sit for 10 minutes to draw out any bitterness. Squeeze the eggplant strips to remove excess liquid; they should turn brown.

Heat the 1 tablespoon of oil in a skillet over medium heat. Add the eggplant and sauté gently for about 5 minutes. Cover and continue to cook for about 4 minutes, until the eggplant is tender.

Transfer the eggplant to a bowl. Add the nori, onion, green onions, Scotch bonnet, thyme, black pepper, and the remaining 1 teaspoon salt. Stir until well combined.

Add the flour, baking powder, and water and stir until well combined. At this point, the mixture can be set aside in the refrigerator for a few hours or fried immediately.

To deep-fry the fritters, heat about 6 inches (15 cm) of oil in a deep, heavy pot over medium-high heat for about 7 minutes. To test whether the oil is hot enough, drop a teaspoonful of the batter into the oil. (Do not forget to remove this small piece of batter from the oil.) If the fritter gets too brown, turn down the heat.

Carefully spoon the batter into the oil, using about 1 heaping teaspoon for each fritter. When you drop each fritter in the oil, make sure the spoon gets coated with oil. This will make the next fritter slide off the spoon more easily. Fry the fritters for 4 minutes, turning them as they bob to the surface. The finished fritters should be golden brown and crispy. (You may need to add more oil to the pot.)

Drain on paper towels and serve warm.

 ISLAND TIP

The batter tends to turn dark if left overnight before frying. It's best to make it no more than 3 or 4 hours before you are ready to fry the fritters. It is possible to shallow-fry instead of deep-frying, but note that this will affect the shape of your fritters. Can they be baked? Yes. Just portion the fritters onto a greased baking sheet and bake at 350°F (180°C) for about 20 to 25 minutes, turning them halfway through the cooking process.

Pholourie (Split Pea Fritters)

These Indian-inspired split pea fritters, widely known as *pholourie* in the Caribbean, are very popular in places like Trinidad and Tobago, Guyana, Suriname, and other Caribbean countries with a large Indo-Caribbean population. Made with a mixture of split pea flour and unbleached flour, these savory bites are great with mango chutney or *kuchela*, a spicy mango condiment available in most West Indian markets. I use them to mop up my curries. They are quite filling, so I tend to serve two per person. You can make them lighter by increasing the amount of water in the batter. You can also add chopped fresh herbs, such as cilantro, to the batter.

1½ cups (190 g) unbleached all-purpose flour

⅓ cup (67 g) yellow split pea flour

2½ teaspoons baking powder

1 teaspoon salt

¼ teaspoon baking soda

2 teaspoons Madras curry powder

1 teaspoon ground cumin

½ teaspoon black pepper

½ teaspoon garam masala

¼ teaspoon cayenne pepper

¼ teaspoon turmeric

4 garlic cloves, pressed

1½ cups (375 ml) water

Canola oil or another neutral-flavored oil

Combine the flours, baking powder, salt, baking soda, curry powder, cumin, black pepper, garam masala, cayenne, turmeric, and garlic. Slowly pour in the water and stir well. The batter should be fairly thick. Cover and let stand for 1 hour to help the batter thicken.

To deep-fry the fritters, heat about 5 inches (13 cm) of oil in a deep, heavy pot over medium-high heat. To test whether the oil is hot enough, drop a teaspoonful of the batter into the oil. (Do not forget to remove this small piece of batter from the oil.) If the fritter gets too brown, turn down the heat.

Carefully spoon the batter into the oil, using about 1 heaping teaspoon for each fritter. When you drop each fritter in the oil, make sure the spoon gets coated with oil.

This will make the next fritter slide off the spoon more easily. Fry the fritters for 4 minutes, turning them as they bob to the surface. The finished fritters should be golden brown and well cooked in the middle.

 **ISLAND TIP**

These freeze well, so make a big batch and save some for the next time you make curry. Just thaw them and then place them in a toaster oven to reheat. You can also reheat them in a regular oven at 350°F (180°C). You can also buy a premade mix for pholourie batter.

Plantain Balls

If you like plantains and you have access to sweet plantains, this recipe is for you. These can be paired with grilled slices of Jerk "Sausage" (page 98) for a sweet and savory mix or dipped into Caribbean Pickle (page 26).

1 overripe plantain

½ teaspoon ground cinnamon

⅛ teaspoon cayenne pepper

⅛ cup (25 g) chopped Everyday Vegan "Ham" (page 100)

¼ cup medium bread crumbs

1 tablespoon nutritional yeast flakes

1 tablespoon wheat germ

¼ teaspoon salt

Large pinch of mild paprika

Preheat the oven to 400°F (200°C) and grease a baking sheet.

Mash the plantain. Stir in the cinnamon, cayenne, and vegan ham. Separately, combine the bread crumbs, nutritional yeast, wheat germ, salt, and paprika and mix well. Put the bread crumb mixture on a plate.

Roll the plantain mixture into walnut-sized balls using a heaping teaspoon to portion out the mixture. Roll them in the breading to coat evenly, and place on the prepared baking sheet. Bake 20 to 25 minutes, until golden brown, turning once during the cooking process.

Spicy Potato Patties

In Caribbean cooking, patties are usually stuffed pastries, but this particular recipe is for an Indian-style shepherd's pie patty that is more like a fritter. You can substitute red lentils or minced seitan for the textured vegetable protein and the flavor will still be good. And if you can't find callaloo, a green, leafy vegetable grown in the Caribbean, you can substitute spinach or another leafy green.

BATTER

1 tablespoon split pea flour

2 tablespoons chickpea flour

3 tablespoons unbleached all-purpose flour

Large pinch of ground cumin

¼ teaspoon salt

¼ teaspoon black pepper

¼ teaspoon mustard powder

¼ to ⅓ cup (62 to 83 ml) water

POTATOES

1 pound, 6 ounces (600 g) potatoes, peeled and chopped

2 tablespoons olive oil

1 onion, minced

1 large garlic clove, minced

1½ teaspoons minced mild chiles, such as Hungarian wax peppers

1 tablespoon black mustard seeds

1 teaspoon ground cumin

1 teaspoon split pea flour

⅛ teaspoon turmeric

1 teaspoon salt, or to taste

FILLING

½ cup (125 ml) boiling water

⅓ cup (33 g) textured vegetable protein (TVP) granules

2 tablespoons canola oil

1 onion, finely chopped

⅛ teaspoon minced Scotch bonnet or habanero pepper

1 garlic clove, minced

1 tablespoon Madras curry powder

¼ teaspoon black pepper

⅛ teaspoon ground nutmeg

1 tablespoon vegan Worcestershire sauce

1 tablespoon Bragg Liquid Aminos or soy sauce

1 tablespoon tomato paste

2 tablespoons water

Canola oil

¾ cup (40 g) panko (Japanese bread crumbs)

Cooked callaloo

1 tablespoon kuchela, optional

Broad-leaf thyme leaves or regular thyme leaves

A few slices of Scotch bonnet or habanero pepper

To make the batter, mix all of the batter ingredients together until well combined. Cover and refrigerate for at least 20 minutes; this will allow the batter to thicken.

To make the potatoes, cook the potatoes in boiling salted water for about 20 minutes, until tender. While the potatoes are cooking, heat the olive oil in a small skillet over medium heat. Add the onion, garlic, mild chiles, and mustard seeds, turn the heat down to low, and sauté for about 5 minutes, until the onion is translucent. Stir in the cumin and remove from the heat. Drain the potatoes, add the split pea flour and turmeric, and mash briefly. Add the contents of the skillet and mix well. Refrigerate for at least 20 minutes to cool down the potato mixture and help it to firm up.

To make the filling, pour the boiling water over the TVP, stir, and cover. Let the TVP hydrate for about 5 minutes. In the meantime, heat canola oil in a skillet over low heat. Add the onion, Scotch bonnet, and garlic and sauté for about 7 minutes, until the onion is tender. Drain the TVP in a fine-mesh sieve and press out any excess water. Add the TVP to the skillet, along with the curry powder, black pepper, nutmeg, Worcestershire sauce, and Bragg Liquid Aminos. Stir well, then stir in the tomato paste and water and cook, stirring occasionally, for 3 minutes.

To assemble the patties, divide the potato mixture into 4 equal parts and use your hands to flatten them into a 4-inch (10 cm) round patty. Place a heaping tablespoon of the filling in the center of each potato patty. Close the patty using your hands to seal off the TVP mixture. Flatten each into a 3½-inch (9 cm) round patty. At this point you can wrap the patties individually in plastic wrap and refrigerate until the next day.

To cook the patties, remove the batter from the fridge and stir to reincorporate the liquid. Heat about ½ inch (1.3 cm) of canola oil in a large, heavy skillet to medium heat. With clean hands, dip each patty into the batter, then coat with an even layer of panko. Test the oil by dropping a little of the panko crumbs into the oil; the oil is ready when they sizzle vigorously. Carefully lower the patties into the oil with a spatula. Fry for 3 minutes, then turn and fry for 3 more minutes. Turn the heat down to medium-low heat and fry for 4 more minutes to ensure that the filling is heated through.

Drain on paper towels. If you aren't serving the patties immediately, place them in a warm oven.

To serve, place one patty in the middle of the plate, spoon cooked callaloo or spinach onto the top of the patty, garnish with Scotch bonnet, then garnish the plate with broad-leaf thyme and dot with kuchela.

 **ISLAND TIP**

Kuchela is a spicy mango condiment available in most West Indian markets. Broad leaf thyme is also known as Cuban oregano or Indian borage and can be cultivated easily, requiring very little care. If this herb is not available, use fresh thyme to garnish the plate.

Breadfruit Chips

Breadfruit chips have been making a comeback in Barbados over the last few years at popular casual dining spots. The taste rivals traditional French fries, but prepare to feel stuffed after eating just two chips.

½ breadfruit
Canola oil
2 teaspoons salt
1 teaspoon green lime zest
½ teaspoon chili powder

Starting with half a fresh breadfruit, cut it in half, peel off the skin, and remove the heart. Slice each piece into crescents. Pat the slices dry.

Heat about ¾ inch (2 cm) of oil in a large, heavy skillet to medium-high heat. Carefully add the breadfruit to the oil and fry for about 3 minutes on each side, until chips are golden brown. If chips are browning too fast reduce heat to medium.

Drain the chips on paper towels. Mix the salt, zest, and chili powder together and sprinkle the mixture over the chips. Serve warm. Dip in ketchup or barbecue sauce.

ISLAND TIP

Canned breadfruit won't work for this dish; you must use fresh. It's available in Asian and Latin American markets in the summertime.

Eggplant Choka

Let us go to South America, to Guyana. Although Guyana lies on the continent of South America, it is the only English-speaking country on the continent, and it is a part of the English-speaking Caribbean. Guyanese cuisine is varied, but one thing that sticks out in my mind is choka. Choka, defined by Cynthia Nelson from her popular blog Tastes Like Home, refers to a method of preparing particular ingredients. It involves fire-roasting, pounding, and grinding. Eggplant Choka is one of my favorite Guyanese choka dishes, with the eggplants fire-roasted for maximum flavor. This dish goes well with Herbed Sada Roti (page 46), or serve it with crackers.

3 small or 1 medium eggplant

2 tablespoons canola oil

1 small onion, chopped

3 garlic cloves, pressed

1 tablespoon mixed chopped herbs (such as marjoram, parsley, or cilantro), green onions, or a combination

½ Scotch bonnet or habanero pepper, seeded and minced

Salt and pepper

To fire-roast the eggplant, prepare an outdoor grill, or use the burner of a gas stove top. Place the eggplant directly on the grill or gas burner, and let the eggplant fire-roast over medium-high heat, turning it periodically for even cooking. Alternatively, if you do not have access to a flame, you can bake the eggplant. Preheat the oven to 350°F (180°C). Wrap the eggplant in foil and bake it until soft, about 45 minutes if using a medium eggplant and 30 minutes if using smaller eggplants. The time of cooking varies with size but a good test to check for doneness is to squeeze the eggplant slightly with tongs, and if it is very soft when squeezed, it is thoroughly cooked. Once the eggplant is very soft, let it stand until cool enough to handle.

Scoop out the eggplant flesh and put it in a bowl, taking care not to get too many pieces of charred eggplant skin into your preparation.

Heat the canola oil in a small skillet over medium heat. Add the onion and garlic and sauté for about 3 minutes, until the onion is translucent. Add the contents of the pan, including the oil, to the eggplant, along with the herbs, and Scotch bonnet. Mash the mixture with a fork until well combined. Season with salt and pepper to taste.

☀ ISLAND TIP

It is a good idea to use small eggplants for this recipe; they will roast more quickly than one larger eggplant. Stove-top roasting or grilling will result in a better flavor than oven roasting, as the eggplant is cooked over an open flame. You can make a slit in each eggplant and put pieces of garlic inside to roast along with the eggplant. When scooping out the eggplant, cover the work surface with newspaper. This makes clean-up very easy.

Féroce d'Avocat
(Cassava Meal with Avocados and Creole Sauce)

I was lucky to spend time with my Saint Lucian grandmother, who brought her style of cooking, including this recipe, to Barbados. When I was a child, this was my favorite dish. It is made with cassava meal and sweet, buttery Caribbean avocados, and topped with Creole Sauce. Cassava meal, also known as farine, is a coarse flour, usually homemade by seasoned farine makers. *Farine* means "flour" in French, so if you go to the markets in Saint Lucia and ask for farine, they will give you coarse cassava flour, or you can request *farine de manioc* or *farine de kassav* if visiting the French West Indies. Making cassava flour is an art that I hope to learn in the future. *Féroce d'avocat* can be translated as "fierceness of an avocado" which probably refers to the heat factor of the dish, especially if made with a lot of Scotch bonnets (though not the case in this recipe). This dish becomes dry and discolored if not consumed immediately, which is why this recipe yields only 2 servings. You can easily multiply it if you want to make more.

> 1 large avocado, or 2 small
> ½ cup (90 g) coarse cassava flour (*farine de manioc* or *kassav*)
> ¼ Scotch bonnet or habanero pepper, minced
> ½ teaspoon salt
> 2 tablespoons canola oil
> ½ cup (125 ml) Creole Sauce (page 36)

Mash the avocado to a pulp. Stir in the cassava flour, then add the Scotch bonnet and salt. Pour the oil over the mixture. This dish will get dry and discolored if it sits, so serve it immediately, topped with the Creole Sauce.

ISLAND TIP

You can serve this dish as an appetizer. Just roll the mixture into little balls, then dip them in Creole Sauce. It also makes a nice accompaniment to Tofish (page 120). You cannot use tapioca flour for cassava flour in this recipe. The cassava used in this recipe is coarse and can be purchased in a West Indian market.

Christophenes Farcis (Stuffed Christophenes)

I have veganized this French West Indies favorite, which is usually offered as an appetizer. The traditional version typically contains meat, and it also relies on bread soaked in milk. In my version, I use a rich roux added to the bread cubes to create additional depth in the flavor.

4 christophenes (chayotes), halved lengthwise and cored

FILLING

⅓ **cup boiling water**

⅓ **cup (70 g) textured vegetable protein (TVP) granules**

1 tablespoon vegan margarine

1 cup (200 g) chopped Everyday Vegan "Ham" (page 100) or smoky vegan sausage

½ **onion, minced**

3 green onions, minced

2 garlic cloves, pressed

¼ **Scotch bonnet or habanero pepper, minced**

¼ **teaspoon white pepper**

1 teaspoon liquid smoke

¼ **teaspoon Angostura bitters, optional**

ROUX

2 tablespoons vegan margarine

3 tablespoons unbleached all-purpose flour

1 cup (250 ml) unsweetened nondairy milk

½ **cup (50 g) bread cubes, preferably whole wheat**

2 tablespoons finely chopped parsley

Salt and black pepper

2 tablespoons grated vegan cheese, optional

2 tablespoons fine bread crumbs

Lightly salt the cavities of the christophenes. Steam them for 30 minutes, until the flesh is tender, replenishing the water if necessary. Remove the christophenes from the steamer to speed cooling.

To make the filling, first hydrate the TVP: Pour the boiling water over the TVP, stir, and cover. Let the TVP hydrate for 5 to 10 minutes. If any liquid remains, drain it off.

Heat the margarine in a skillet over medium heat. Stir in the TVP, vegan ham, onion, green onions, garlic, Scotch bonnet, white pepper, liquid smoke, and optional bitters. Sauté for 4 minutes, until the onions are translucent and the ham and TVP are slightly browned.

To make the roux, heat the margarine in a small saucepan over medium heat. Sprinkle in the flour, whisking continuously. Slowly pour in the nondairy milk, still whisking continuously to prevent any lumps from forming. Cook, whisking from time to time, for about 3 to 5 minutes, until the roux thickens. Add the bread and parsley and stir until well combined. Season with salt and black pepper to taste.

Preheat the oven to 400°F (200°C) and grease a large baking pan.

Once the christophenes are cool enough to handle, scoop out most of the flesh from each half, leaving an intact shell. Put the christophene flesh in a bowl and mash to a pulp.

Layer the fillings in the christophenes in the following order: half of the roux and bread mixture, all of the mashed christophene, half of the TVP mixture, the remaining roux, and the remaining TVP mixture. Use your hands and pack the filling in tight. Sprinkle the optional cheese over the top, then dust with the bread crumbs. Put the christophenes in a baking pan. Bake for 20 minutes, until filling starts to meld together. Turn on the broiler to high heat and broil for 3 minutes, until the tops are lightly browned. Serve warm.

 ISLAND TIP

Some christophenes (chayotes) are sold particularly ripe, with a beige skin, and these work well in this recipe. You could use ¾ cup minced seitan in place of the TVP if you like. Note that you do not need vegan cheese to enjoy this dish, as it is rich on its own. You can also use the filling without the roux to stuff tomatoes, in which case the dish is known as tomato *farci* (French for "stuffed"). And you can also eat the skin of the christophene.

Curried Potato Salad

In the Caribbean, we usually make a standard U.S.–style potato salad and add some mixed vegetables to it. I created this recipe back when I was a teenager. While I was working on this book, my mother mailed me the tattered piece of paper I had originally written it on. This salad uses a vinaigrette for seasoning, so the vegan mayonnaise is optional.

1¼ pounds (550 g) potatoes, cut into ¾-inch (2 cm) cubes

¼ cup olive oil (62 ml)

2 tablespoons canola oil or olive oil

2 tablespoons distilled white vinegar

1 teaspoon apple cider vinegar

1 tablespoon water

2 teaspoons salt

1½ teaspoons Madras curry powder

1 onion, minced

2 garlic cloves, pressed

¼ red bell pepper, finely chopped

¼ green bell pepper, finely chopped

⅛ teaspoon chopped Scotch bonnet or habanero pepper minced, optional

2 to 3 tablespoons finely chopped fresh dill, or 2 to 3 teaspoons dried

¼ cup (62 ml) vegan mayonnaise, optional

Cook the potatoes in boiling salted water for about 8 to 10 minutes, until tender but still firm enough to hold their shape. Drain and cool to room temperature.

Combine the oils, vinegars, water, salt, curry powder, onion, garlic, bell peppers, Scotch bonnet, and dill and whisk until thoroughly combined. Put the potatoes in a shallow container and pour in the dressing. Stir gently, taking care not to break up the potatoes. Cover and refrigerate for 30 minutes. Stir in mayonnaise, if using, with a fork to ensure intact potatoes.

 **ISLAND TIP**

You can leave the skins on the potatoes if you like. For vegan mayonnaise, I use Nasoya Nayonaise or Spectrum Light Canola Mayo.

Christophene, Carrot, and Green Bean Salad

SERVES 4

Christophene (also known outside the Caribbean as chayote) is widely available. On various islands this mixture of vegetables is usually served as a cooked vegetable side at Sunday lunch. This recipe makes use of a vinaigrette to enhance the flavors of the vegetables. Even though the amount of mild red chiles is small, be sure to include it. The color will enhance the appearance of the dish.

- **2 christophenes (chayotes), peeled, seeds removed, and cut into crescents**
- **1 carrot, peeled and cut into sticks**
- **½ cup cut green beans, chopped in half**
- **½ cup (125 ml) distilled white vinegar**
- **2 tablespoons canola oil**
- **¼ onion, minced**
- **2 garlic cloves, minced**
- **¼ teaspoon minced Scotch bonnet or habanero pepper, optional**
- **1 teaspoon chopped mild red chile peppers, such as Hungarian wax peppers**
- **1 tablespoon finely chopped parsley**
- **2 tablespoons brown sugar**
- **½ teaspoon salt**
- **½ teaspoon black pepper**

Steam the christophene, carrot, and green beans for 25 minutes, until they are tender but not too soft. Let them cool to room temperature before mixing them in the vinaigrette.

Put the vinegar, oil, onion, garlic, optional Scotch bonnet, mild chiles, parsley, sugar, salt, and black pepper in a bowl large enough to hold the vegetables. Whisk until thoroughly combined. Add the vegetables and toss with the dressing. Serve at room temperature or cold.

 **ISLAND TIP**

If you like some of your vegetables crisp-tender, cook the carrots for a shorter time. This creates more texture in the salad.

Caribbean Coleslaw

I know you must be expecting a new coleslaw recipe, but I will not lie to you: Caribbean coleslaw is just like U.S.–style coleslaw. Raisins and chopped apples appear in coleslaw in many Caribbean households now due to the cultural exchange between the Caribbean and the United States. I include this recipe because coleslaw helps to balance out spicy dishes, which are plentiful in this book. It is especially good with Curried TVP Stew (page 87) and Island Burgers (page 114).

1 carrot, coarsely grated
¼ cabbage, cut into very thin strips
⅓ cup (80 ml) vegan mayonnaise
1½ teaspoons brown sugar, or ½ teaspoon agave nectar
¼ teaspoon black pepper
1 teaspoon minced onion, optional
½ teaspoon minced parsley, optional

Put all of the ingredients in a bowl and stir until well combined. Serve chilled.

ISLAND TIP

You can grate the carrots and cabbage as fine or as coarse as you wish for this recipe. If they are fine, the coleslaw will be creamier. If they are coarse, the coleslaw will be crunchy and fresh tasting. For vegan mayonnaise, I like Nasoya Nayonaise or Spectrum Light Canola Mayo.

SOUPS
AND STEWS

CONTRARY TO POPULAR belief, soups are common in the Caribbean. Despite the hot climate, many people enjoy a hearty soup. Most Caribbean soups are chunky, consisting of root vegetables such as sweet potatoes, yams, and dasheen (also known as taro). Chunks of pumpkin are often added to give body. Blended or pureed soups such as split pea soup are also popular. Some Caribbean soups use a bit of smoked meat as a base flavor. Where I wanted to create that effect, I've included liquid smoke or Everyday Vegan "Ham" (page 100) in the recipe.

The stews in this book are high in protein and can be paired with some of the sides in chapter 6 or any carbohydrate of your choice.

Caribbean Green Split Pea Soup

SERVES 4

I've veganized this classic bean soup with the help of Everyday Vegan "Ham" (page 100). It is terrific with crusty bread.

2 tablespoons olive oil

1 shallot, finely chopped

1 onion, finely chopped

1 garlic clove, finely chopped

1 celery stalk, finely chopped

1¼ cups (250 g) dried green split peas, soaked overnight or quick-soaked (see Island Tip)

2 teaspoons Bajan Seasoning (page 19)

4½ cups (1.1 liters) water

¼ teaspoon minced fresh thyme, or a pinch of dried

¼ teaspoon minced fresh basil, or ⅛ teaspoon dried

¼ Scotch bonnet pepper, minced

2 tablespoons nutritional yeast flakes

1 teaspoon seasoning salt

1 teaspoon onion powder

¼ teaspoon chili powder

¼ teaspoon black pepper

½ cup (100 g) chopped Everyday Vegan "Ham" (page 100) or smoky vegan sausage

1 teaspoon liquid smoke

1 teaspoon salt, or to taste

Heat the olive oil in a soup pot over medium heat. Add the shallot, onion, garlic, and celery and sauté for 5 minutes, until the vegetables are tender. Stir in the split peas, Bajan Seasoning, and 2 cups (500 ml) of the water. Cover and cook over medium heat for 15 minutes.

Add the thyme, basil, Scotch bonnet, nutritional yeast, seasoning salt, onion powder, chili powder, and black pepper. Cover and cook for 20 minutes.

Add another 2 cups (500 ml) of the water. Mix the vegan ham and liquid smoke together, then add it to the soup. Turn the heat down to medium-low, cover, and cook for about 40 minutes, or until the peas are tender. Let the soup cool slightly.

Working in batches, transfer the soup to a food processor or blender (or use an immersion blender) and process until smooth. Return the soup to the pot and stir in the remaining ½ cup (100 ml) of water. Taste, adjust the salt, and add a few more drops of liquid smoke if you like. Heat the soup back up and serve it hot.

☀ ISLAND TIP

To quick-soak the split peas, add enough boiling water to cover by about 2 inches (5 cm) and let them sit for about 20 minutes. The vegan ham can be blended in the soup, or for a chunkier version, add it after you've pureed the soup. And if you like chunky soups, you don't have to blend the soup at all.

Creamy Pumpkin Soup

In the West Indies, pumpkin soup is usually of a spicy nature, but some restaurants offer a milder soup like this one. Calabaza squash is another name for West Indian pumpkin, but you can use kabocha squash if you can't find calabaza.

1 tablespoon vegan margarine or olive oil

7 ounces (200 g) orange-fleshed sweet potato, chopped

12 ounces (350 g) calabaza (West Indian) squash, kabocha squash, or any other winter squash

½ onion, finely chopped

6 garlic cloves, minced

3 cups (750 ml) water

1 teaspoon salt

1 teaspoon black pepper

¼ to ½ teaspoon ground cloves

¼ teaspoon ground allspice

¼ teaspoon ground nutmeg

⅛ teaspoon ground ginger or minced fresh ginger

⅛ teaspoon ground cinnamon

1 teaspoon finely chopped fresh rosemary, or ½ teaspoon dried

1 teaspoon finely chopped fresh thyme, or ¼ teaspoon dried

½ cup (125 ml) vegetable stock, unsalted

⅓ cup (75 ml) nondairy creamer or unsweetened nondairy milk

1 teaspoon agave nectar

Heat the margarine in a soup pot over medium heat. Add the sweet potato, squash, onion, and 3 of the garlic cloves and sauté for 5 minutes. Stir in the water, salt, pepper, cloves, allspice, nutmeg, ginger, cinnamon, and rosemary. Cover and cook for 25 to 30 minutes, until the vegetables are tender. Let the soup cool slightly.

Stir in the remaining 3 garlic cloves and the thyme and stock. Using an immersion blender or a food processor, blend the soup until smooth. Heat the soup back up and taste for salt and pepper. Stir in the nondairy creamer and agave nectar and cook for 1 minute. Serve hot.

Highlights from a Caribbean Produce Aisle

a. Breadfruit
b. Cassava
c. Sweet potatoes
d. Yams
e. Plantains
f. Scotch bonnet peppers
g. Green onions

Bajan Seasoning • page 19

Saint Lucian Bakes • page 41

Eggplant and Seaweed Accras • page 60

Bajan "Beef" Stew • page 85, with Pigeon Pea Rice • page 157

Lentil Patties • page 110

Island Burger • page 114

Cou-Cou and Tofish • page 120, **with Creole Sauce** • page 36

Vegan Steamed Pudding and Souse • page 118

Jerk Pizza with Sweet Potato Crust • page 128

7

Trinidadian Doubles • page 112

STEP 1 Stretch dough balls (holes are OK).

STEP 2 Frying bara.

STEP 3 Fried bara.

STEP 4 Overlapped bara with filling.

STEP 5 Bara with filling and condiment.

STEP 6 Fold doubles in paper and serve.

Barbadian Coconut Turnovers • page 186

STEP 1 Roll each piece of dough into a circular shape with a diameter of 4½ to 5 inches (11–13 cm).

STEP 2 Spoon filling into the center of each dough circle.

STEP 3 Fold each circle in half over the filling.

STEP 4 Seal each circle of dough, pressing its edges together to ensure filling stays inside.

STEP 5 Sealed dough.

STEP 6 Form sealed circles of dough into a miniature loaf shape.

STEP 7 Dough in mini-loaf shape.

STEP 8 Place turnovers in greased pans.

STEP 9 Brush sugar-water onto turnovers, and sprinkle coarse sugar on top.

STEP 10 Turnovers baked to perfection.

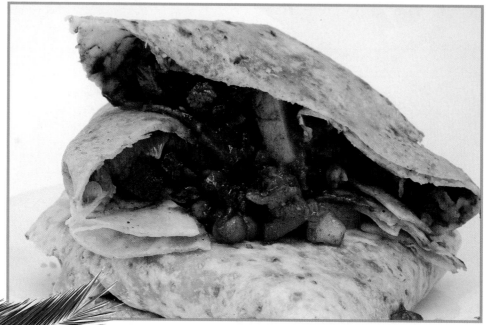

Dal Puri Roti • page 145, stuffed with Curried Potatoes and Pumpkin • page 150, and Curried TVP Stew • page 87

STEP 1 Form dough into a cup shape.

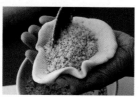

STEP 2 Add filling to dough cup.

STEP 3 Seal dough cup at edges.

STEP 4 Form dough into a ball.

STEP 5 Seal roti.

STEP 6 Slightly flatten roti.

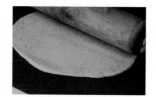

STEP 7 Roll stuffed roti into a thin tortilla shape.

STEP 8 Cook roti skin on tawa or griddle surface.

STEP 9 Fill roti skin with Curried Potatoes and Pumpkin, then add TVP Stew.

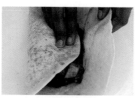

STEP 11 Fold outer edges of roti skin over filling.

STEP 12 Fold over ends of roti skin.

STEP 13 Wrap roti into square shape.

Buss-Up-Shut Roti • page 147

STEP 1 Cut dough into six equal pieces.

STEP 2 Roll each piece of dough out into a shape with a diameter of at least five inches.

STEP 3 Cut the dough once from the center to an edge.

STEP 4 Roll the dough into a cone shape.

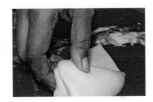

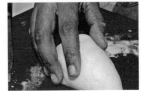

STEP 5 Dough cone.

STEP 6 Push in the tip of the cone.

STEP 7 Formed roll.

STEP 8 Let rise for 45 minutes.

Bajan Macaroni Pie with Tofu Cheddar • page 124

Classic Barbadian Sweet Potato Pie • page 149

Okra in Sofrito Sauce • page 163

Conkies • page 191

Coconut Bread • page 174

Rum Cake • page 194

Rum Punch • page 223

Sugar Cakes • page 206

Bajan Soup with Dumplings

In the Caribbean, soup isn't reserved for rainy days. It can be served anytime, even on the most scorching of days. Women with makeshift restaurants cook up huge pots of this and sell it on the streets or in mobile restaurants, and even children get excited about this midweek soup. This recipe uses white sweet potatoes and pigeon peas as the base. Served with hearty spiced dumplings, this will please most soup lovers— and big appetites. Barbadians always say, "A soup without dumplings is not a soup." I don't entirely agree with that, but the dumplings do really work well with this soup.

SOUP

1 heaping tablespoon vegan margarine

1 onion, finely chopped

½ cup (85 g) fresh, frozen, or canned pigeon peas

½ bell pepper, any color, finely chopped

1 carrot, coarsely chopped

1 celery stalk, sliced

4 okra pods, thinly sliced

9 ounces (250 g) calabaza squash, kabocha squash, or any other winter squash, chopped

11 ounces (300 g) white sweet potato, chopped

5¼ cups (1.25 liters) water

1 teaspoon adobo seasoning

1 teaspoon salt

½ teaspoon celery salt

1 Scotch bonnet pepper or habanero pepper

2 garlic cloves, thinly sliced

1 teaspoon nutritional yeast flakes

½ teaspoon black pepper

¼ teaspoon Bajan Pepper Sauce (page 19)

Bouquet garni (see page 5) made with 2 green onions, a few sprigs each of fresh thyme and marjoram, and a few stems of parsley

¼ cup chopped (50 g) Everyday Vegan "Ham" (page 100), optional

DUMPLINGS

1¼ cups (150 g) whole wheat flour

½ teaspoon salt

¼ teaspoon ground cinnamon or cassia

⅛ teaspoon ground nutmeg

1½ tablespoons vegan margarine

1¼ cups (156 ml) unsweetened nondairy milk

½ teaspoon baking powder

1 teaspoon brown sugar

To make the soup, heat the margarine in a soup pot over medium heat. Add the onion, peas, bell pepper, carrot, celery, and okra and sauté for a few minutes, until the vegetables are slightly tender. Add the squash and sweet potato, then stir in the water, adobo seasoning, salt, and celery salt. Add the Scotch bonnet, garlic, nutritional yeast, black pepper, and pepper sauce, then add the bouquet garni and stir gently. Lower the heat to medium-low and cook, stirring occasionally, for about 25 minutes.

Meanwhile, make the dumplings. Mix the flour, salt, cinnamon, and nutmeg together in a bowl. Add the margarine and rub it into the flour using your fingertips. Stir in the nondairy milk, baking powder, and sugar until well incorporated into the flour mixture. Form the dough into 8 round dumplings. Add the dumplings to the soup and cook the soup for 15 more minutes. The soup should be yellowish in color, and the texture should be slightly thick, not thin like a broth. Remove and discard the bouquet garni. Serve the soup hot, being sure to divide the dumplings evenly among the servings.

☀ ISLAND TIP

Add cubes of seitan or another meat substitute to make the soup a complete meal. You can make the dumplings with unbleached all-purpose flour if you like.

Lentil Stew

SERVES 4

Lentil stew is already a classic in most vegan and vegetarian kitchens but mine is a little different. I've spiced it up with Caribbean seasonings and colored it dark brown with Caribbean Caramel. A side of rice would be the perfect accompaniment.

1 tablespoon canola oil

1 onion, chopped

2 teaspoons Madras curry powder

1 teaspoon mild paprika

½ teaspoon ground cumin

¾ cup (150 g) dried brown lentils, soaked overnight or quick-soaked (see Island Tip), and drained

3 cups (750 ml) water, or more as needed

3 tablespoons Bragg Liquid Aminos or soy sauce

1 tablespoon tomato paste

1 heaping tablespoon Bajan Seasoning (page 19)

½ teaspoon Caribbean Caramel (page 25) or browning

2 tablespoons nutritional yeast flakes

Salt and pepper

Heat the canola oil in a large saucepan over medium heat. Add the onion and sauté for 3 minutes, until translucent. Stir in the curry powder, paprika, and cumin, then stir in the lentils, water, Bragg Liquid Aminos, tomato paste, Bajan Seasoning, Caribbean Caramel, and nutritional yeast. Turn the heat down to medium-low, cover, and cook, stirring occasionally, for about 35 to 40 minutes, until the lentils are tender. Add extra water if the stew gets too dry or starts to stick.

Season with salt and pepper to taste, and serve hot.

ISLAND TIP

To quick-soak the lentils, add enough boiling water to cover by about 2 inches and let them sit for about 20 minutes. You can make a lentil version of shepherd's pie with this stew. Just spread it in an even layer in a baking pan, top with mashed potatoes, and bake at 400°F (200°C) until the dish is heated through and the potatoes are lightly browned.

Bajan "Beef" Stew

On some islands, the meat version of this stew is made on Sundays or special occasions. It's also sometimes offered as a street food. The TVP can be marinated overnight to save time, and with this recipe marinating overnight gives a more flavorful stew. If you have leftovers, keep in mind that the liquid will be absorbed into the TVP, so you may want to add some water when reheating.

> 1½ cups boiling water
>
> 1½ cups (200 g) textured vegetable protein (TVP) chunks
>
> 2 heaping tablespoons Bajan Seasoning (page 19), plus 1 teaspoon, optional
>
> 1 tablespoon Marmite or Vegemite
>
> 2 tablespoons oil
>
> 1 small onion, chopped
>
> 1 carrot, diced small
>
> 1 potato, diced small
>
> ½ teaspoon mild paprika
>
> ½ teaspoon black pepper
>
> 4¼ cups (1 liter) water
>
> 1 to 2 tablespoons Bragg Liquid Aminos or soy sauce
>
> 2 tablespoons ketchup
>
> 1 tablespoon tomato paste
>
> 1 tablespoon Caribbean Caramel (page 25) or browning
>
> 1 tablespoon vegan Worcestershire sauce
>
> 1 teaspoon cornstarch
>
> 1 garlic clove, pressed
>
> ¼ teaspoon Bajan Pepper Sauce (page 23), optional

Pour just enough boiling water over the TVP to cover it. Let the TVP hydrate for 5 to 10 minutes.

If any liquid remains, drain most of it off. Add 2 heaping tablespoons of Bajan Seasoning, stir well, then add the Marmite. Marinate for at least 15 minutes, or as long as overnight.

Heat the oil in a soup pot over medium heat. Add the onion, carrot, and potato and sauté for 5 minutes, until the onions are translucent. Stir in the TVP, paprika, and pepper and cook for 5 minutes, stirring occasionally. Stir in the water. Turn the heat down to low, cover, and simmer for 30 minutes.

Stir in the Bragg Liquid Aminos, ketchup, tomato paste, Caribbean Caramel, and Worcestershire sauce, cover, and cook for 10 minutes. Stir the cornstarch into a bit of water, then add it to the pot, along with the garlic. Increase the heat to medium and cook uncovered, stirring occasionally, for about 5 to 7 minutes, until thick. If using the optional pepper sauce and Bajan Seasoning, stir them in and cook for 5 more minutes. Taste and adjust the saltiness by adding more Bragg Liquid Aminos, if you like.

Curried TVP Stew

SERVES 4 IF ACCOMPANIED BY RICE, OR 6 IF USED AS ROTI FILLING

This flavorful stew can be served as a main course alongside a rice dish. You can also use it as a filling for roti, following the method in Dal Puri Roti (page 145) and Buss-Up-Shut Roti (page 147). If you like, you can use about 1 cup of a meat substitute such as Morningstar Farms Meal Starters Chick'n Strips in place of the TVP. Just chop it into chunks and marinate it as you would the TVP. This stew freezes well.

2 tablespoons Bajan Seasoning (page 19)

1 tablespoon Marmite or Vegemite

2 tablespoons Bragg Liquid Aminos

½ cup textured vegetable protein (TVP) chunks

3 tablespoons canola oil

2½ tablespoons Madras curry powder

½ teaspoon garam masala

1 onion, chopped

One 15.5-ounce (439 g) can chickpeas, drained and rinsed

1 cup (250 ml) water

1 teaspoon salt

1 teaspoon dried thyme

1 teaspoon mild paprika

½ teaspoon black pepper

½ cup (125 ml) tomato sauce or ketchup

½ teaspoon Bajan Pepper Sauce (page 23)

Hydrate TVP with just enough hot water to cover the TVP. Let this stand for 10 to 15 minutes before using. If any liquid remains, drain most of it off. Mix the Bajan Seasoning, Marmite, and Bragg Liquid Aminos together in a shallow pan. Add the TVP and marinate for 20 minutes.

Heat the oil in a large saucepan over medium heat. Stir in the curry powder and garam masala, then add the onion and stir to coat with the spiced oil. Stir in the TVP, along with its marinade, then add the chickpeas and water. Lower the heat, cover, and simmer gently for about 15 minutes.

Add the salt, thyme, paprika, pepper, tomato sauce, and pepper sauce. Reduce the heat to medium low. Continue to simmer for about 20 to 25 minutes, until the liquid has reduced to a slightly thick dark sauce clinging to the TVP.

Chickpea Curry

This bold, spicy curry is quick and easy to make, so it is a good choice for busy afternoons and evenings. For a colorful presentation, serve it with Spinach Rice (page 136). It is also an excellent filling for or accompaniment with Dal Puri Roti (page 145) or Buss-Up-Shut Roti (page 147).

2 tablespoons olive oil

1 onion, finely chopped

1 carrot, diced small

2 tablespoons Colombo or Madras curry powder

1½ teaspoons ground cumin

Two 15.5-ounce (439 g) cans chickpeas, drained and rinsed

2½ cups (625 ml) water, or more as needed

1½ teaspoons tomato paste

1½ teaspoons American-style prepared mustard

**½ teaspoon Bajan Pepper Sauce (page 23),
    or ⅛ to ¼ teaspoon cayenne pepper**

1 teaspoon salt

1 teaspoon turmeric

½ teaspoon black pepper

½ teaspoon mild paprika

¼ teaspoon garam masala

3 to 4 garlic cloves, pressed

Heat the oil in a large saucepan over medium heat. Add the onion, carrot, curry powder, and cumin and sauté for about 5 minutes, until the onion is slightly translucent. Stir in the chickpeas and water and cook for 15 minutes.

Stir in the tomato paste, mustard, pepper sauce, salt, turmeric, pepper, paprika, and garam masala. Turn the heat down to low, cover, and simmer for 30 minutes.

Add the garlic and simmer uncovered, stirring occasionally for 5 to 7 minutes, until thick. Add a bit more water if the stew gets too thick. Serve hot.

ISLAND TIP

Do not worry about the tomato paste ruining the color of your curry. At the end of its slow cooking, the curry is not red at all—it is bright orange.

Mixed Bean Stew

Recently, I learned that Ital food, eaten by Rastafarians, is based on using organic ingredients and foods in their natural state. Some Rastafarians avoid using salt and rely only on herbs, spices, and aromatic vegetables to flavor the food. The juice from celery is a good replacement for salt. I've made this dish salt free. You can salt it if you like, but taste it without salt first, because it is full of flavor from the spices and fresh herbs. I developed this recipe using a combination of pigeon peas, lentils, black-eyed peas, split peas, and red beans, but you can use whatever dried beans you have on hand. To decrease the cooking time and make the beans more tender, it's a good idea to soak them overnight, so plan ahead.

2 tablespoons olive oil or coconut oil

1 onion, chopped

4 garlic cloves, pressed

2 tablespoons chopped mild chile peppers, such as Hungarian wax peppers

1 tomato, coarsely chopped

⅓ cup mixed minced herbs (such as basil, marjoram, parsley, or thyme), green onions, or a combination

4 green onions, finely chopped

1 large celery stalk, finely chopped

1 carrot, diced small

1 teaspoon minced ginger

1½ tablespoons Madras curry powder

1½ teaspoons ground cumin

1 teaspoon black pepper

¼ teaspoon garam masala

1 cup (about 230 g) mixed dried beans, soaked overnight and drained

3¼ cups (750 ml) water

1 cup (250 ml) tomato sauce

1 teaspoon Bajan Pepper Sauce (page 23)

1 teaspoon fresh rosemary leaves, or ½ teaspoon dried

1 Scotch bonnet or habanero pepper, seeded and chopped

2 tablespoons chopped parsley

1 teaspoon mild paprika

1 bay leaf, optional

Heat the oil in a large saucepan over medium heat. Add the onion, garlic, mild chiles, tomato, herbs, green onion, celery, carrots, ginger, curry powder, cumin, black pepper, and garam masala and sauté for 5 minutes. Stir in the beans, water, tomato sauce, pepper sauce, rosemary, Scotch bonnet, parsley, paprika, and optional bay leaf. Lower the heat, cover, and simmer, stirring occasionally, for about 1 hour, until the beans are soft. Add a little water if necessary near the end of the cooking time, if the stew has become too thick.

 **ISLAND TIP**

Dried red beans and black-eyed peas are quite hard and need to be soaked well before using them in this stew. If you're short on time, use softer beans and peas, such as pigeon peas, lentils, and split peas, which cook well after a quick soak.

Fat-Free Black-Eyed Pea Stew

A fat-free stew is just what you need when you are getting over a cold, and this dish is also the perfect thing to make when you want to put something extra-nutritious into your body. But bean stews, especially fat-free versions, have a tendency to just taste like bean if you don't use the right herbs and spices. Black-eyed peas have a distinct flavor that I love, and if you love it too, don't rinse the beans too much, or you will lose that flavor.

One 15-ounce can (439 ml) black-eyed peas, drained
1 cup (250 ml) water
½ onion, finely chopped
2 garlic cloves, minced
1 carrot, diced small
3 tomatoes, chopped
2 green onions, minced
2 tablespoons chopped fresh basil, or 2 teaspoons dried
½ teaspoon chopped fresh thyme, or ⅛ teaspoon dried
1 teaspoon mild paprika
1 teaspoon Madras curry powder
1 teaspoon salt
½ teaspoon black pepper
1 to 2 tablespoons ketchup
1 tablespoon tomato paste
1½ tablespoons Bajan Seasoning (page 19)
1 teaspoon vegan Worcestershire sauce
1 teaspoon Angostura bitters, optional
½ teaspoon Bajan Pepper Sauce (page 23), optional

Put all of the ingredients in a pot or pressure cooker and stir them together. Cook in a pot over low heat for 35 minutes, or in a pressure cooker at medium-low pressure for 35 minutes. Serve hot.

 **ISLAND TIP**

If you use dried black-eyed peas in this dish, make sure you soak them for a full day before cooking them, changing the water periodically.

Yellow Split Pea Dal

You have made dal, but there's a good chance you haven't made it this way. The split peas are tossed with oil, baking powder (which helps speed up cooking time), and turmeric, then boiled. Spices, onions, and hot peppers are added halfway through the cooking, then sautéed garlic and cumin seeds are added at the end of cooking. The result is a creamy, hearty dal that's full of flavor. Serve it on plain basmati rice or with Buss-Up-Shut Roti (page 147).

6¼ cups (1.5 liters) water, divided

1½ cups (300 g) dried yellow or green split peas, picked over and rinsed

2 tablespoons coconut oil or canola oil

½ teaspoon baking powder

½ teaspoon turmeric

1 tablespoon Madras curry powder

1 teaspoon ground cumin

½ teaspoon garam masala

1 onion, finely chopped

3 green onions, minced

½ Scotch bonnet or habanero pepper, seeded and minced

1½ teaspoons salt

4 garlic cloves, minced

1 teaspoon cumin seeds

Bring 3¾ cups (875 ml) of the water to a boil in a soup pot. Combine the peas, 1 tablespoon of the oil, and the baking powder and turmeric. Add the mixture to the boiling water. Turn the heat down to medium, cover, and cook for 20 minutes.

Stir in the curry powder, cumin, and garam masala, then stir in 2 more cups (500 ml) of the water. Cover and cook for 10 minutes.

Stir in the onion, green onion, Scotch bonnet, and salt, then stir in the remaining ½ cup (125 ml) water. Cook, stirring occasionally to prevent sticking, for 15 minutes. If at this stage the dal looks a little too thick, add in an extra ½ cup (125 ml) of water.

Heat the remaining tablespoon of oil in a small skillet over medium heat. Add the garlic and cumin seeds and sauté for 3 minutes, until garlic is slightly brown. Scrape the contents of the pan into the dal. Stir well. Taste and adjust the salt if necessary.

☀ ISLAND TIP

Green split peas have a more robust flavor. I prefer the delicate flavor of yellow, so that's what I call for here. If you have green split peas, you can use them, but eventually try it both ways to see which you like best. You can also mix green and yellow split peas, but in my experience the green tend to cook faster, so keep that in mind.

Creole Red Bean Stew

Creole beans are served as a side dish in the French West Indies. Sometimes the dish is made with beurre rouge (French for "red butter") for more color. Although classic beurre rouge is made with butter and red wine, in the French West Indies this preparation is vegan, as it applies to oil heated with annatto seeds to infuse it with color. Because this recipe uses canned beans, it comes together quickly.

1 tablespoon olive oil

½ onion, chopped

2 green onions, finely chopped

2 garlic cloves, minced

½ green bell pepper, chopped

One 15.5-ounce (439 g) can red beans, drained and rinsed

1 teaspoon ground cumin

½ teaspoon chili powder

½ cup (125 ml) water

One 8-ounce (227 g) can tomato sauce, preferably Spanish-style

1 tablespoon Bragg Liquid Aminos or soy sauce

1 tablespoon Bajan Seasoning (page 19) or Trinidadian Green Seasoning (page 22)

1 teaspoon American-style prepared mustard

1 teaspoon vegan Worcestershire sauce

2 small mild chile peppers, such as Hungarian wax peppers, chopped, optional

Heat the oil in a large saucepan over medium heat. Add the onion, green onions, garlic, and bell pepper and sauté for 2 minutes, until vegetables are slightly tender. Stir in the beans, cumin, chili powder, water, tomato sauce, Bragg Liquid Aminos, Bajan Seasoning, mustard, Worcestershire sauce, and optional mild chiles. Cook, stirring occasionally, for 5 minutes. Serve warm.

 ISLAND TIP

For the best flavor in this dish, use a Spanish-style tomato sauce. I like Goya brand. If you venture to the French West Indies, keep in mind that Creole beans are usually cooked with smoked meat, so clarify that before you order the dish.

ENTRÉES

FOR ME, CARIBBEAN entrées are comfort foods, and they have every right to be this way. Families would bond during mealtime, and whoever cooked the meal, be it the mother or father or someone else, felt a sense of pride in providing quality meals for their family.

Curry is a main dish that is sometimes made in Caribbean households, particularly in Guyana and Trinidad and Tobago. Curry is often served with roti and rice. You'll find roti recipes on pages 46, 145, and 147, and many rice dishes in chapter 6.

In Barbados, pasta and rice dishes are popular with dark spicy stews colored with burnt sugar. Countries in the eastern Caribbean, such as Saint Lucia, Saint Vincent, and the Grenadines, have large agricultural bases and some of their dishes include ground provisions like yams, green bananas, breadfruit, and dasheen (which is also known as taro in some places, though not in the Caribbean).

Jerk "Sausages"

These sausages are soft, tender, and juicy, and have a slightly fruity flavor. You can make them as spicy or as mild as you like. The method of cooking is a simple steam in aluminum foil, a technique made popular by cookbook author and food blogger Julie Hasson. Once cooked and cooled, the sausage can be grilled or fried and coated with additional sauces. If you use commercial vegan sausages, this version may be softer than what you are used to. But if you freeze them, you can then slice or crumble them easily. Wear gloves when mixing and shaping the sausage, as there are Scotch bonnets in the jerk seasoning. The tamarind extract is optional, but it gives the sausage a nice tang.

1 cup (400 g) canned or cooked white beans, drained and rinsed

¾ cup (150 g) firm tofu, crumbled

1¼ cups (250 ml) water

½ cup (125 ml) tomato sauce

½ cup (125 ml) Bragg Liquid Aminos or soy sauce

¼ cup (62 ml) olive oil

¼ cup (62 ml) pineapple juice or crushed pineapple

¼ cup (62 ml) Jamaican Jerk Seasoning (page 20)

2 to 3 tablespoons American-style prepared mustard

1 teaspoon Marmite or Vegemite

1 teaspoon tamarind extract, optional

3 tablespoons brown sugar

1 tablespoon salt

1 tablespoon nutritional yeast flakes

1 tablespoon dried thyme

1 tablespoon onion powder

1 teaspoon mild paprika

½ teaspoon ground nutmeg

Large pinch of cayenne pepper

1 shallot, minced

2½ cups (350 g) gluten flour

Put the beans and tofu in a blender or food processor. Pour in ¼ cup of water and process until smooth. Transfer to a bowl and add 1 cup of water, along with the tomato sauce, liquid aminos, olive oil, pineapple juice, jerk seasoning, mustard, Marmite, tamarind extract, sugar, salt, nutritional yeast, thyme, onion powder, paprika, nutmeg, cayenne, and shallot. Stir until thoroughly combined. Add the gluten flour and mix well. You may find it easiest to use your hands at this point. Do not forget to wear gloves.

Cut twelve 9-inch (23 cm) squares of aluminum foil. Divide the sausage mixture in 12 equal pieces and roll each into a 6-inch (15 cm) sausage between your hands. Roll each sausage tightly in foil and secure the ends by twisting the foil.

Steam the sausages for 1½ hours, replenishing the water as needed. Cool the sausages before preparing them; this will help them firm up.

 **ISLAND TIP**

If you're using the Jamaican Jerk Seasoning, which is mild, and you prefer a spicy sausage, puree part of a Scotch bonnet pepper or the whole pepper, including the seeds, with the beans. For sliceable sausage, freeze it and then, a little while before you're ready to cook, thaw it briefly. This makes it easy to cut the sausage into rounds or strips. To prepare the sausage for a sandwich or salad, unwrap it and lightly fry it in a little vegetable oil over medium heat until crispy on the outside.

Everyday Vegan "Ham"

This vegan ham, made from seitan, is like a fine wine: It gets better with age. It is a go-to recipe in this book because it serves as a replacement for smoked sausage in many recipes. It is reminiscent of a traditional Caribbean Christmas ham, seasoned with pineapple juice, cloves, and brown sugar. It can be eaten cold or sautéed.

1 cup (120 g) gluten flour

1 teaspoon salt

½ teaspoon black pepper

¼ teaspoon mild paprika

¼ teaspoon ground cloves

¼ cup (62 ml) water

2 tablespoons maple syrup

2 tablespoons pineapple juice

2 tablespoons plus 1 teaspoon canola oil

1 tablespoon liquid smoke

1 tablespoon Bragg Liquid Aminos or soy sauce

1 tablespoon tomato paste

¼ teaspoon Angostura bitters, optional

1 to 2 garlic cloves, pressed, optional

Put the gluten flour, salt, peppper, paprika, and cloves in a bowl and stir until well combined. Separately, mix the water, maple syrup, juice, oil, liquid smoke, Bragg Liquid Aminos, tomato paste, optional bitters, and optional garlic together. Pour the wet mixture into the gluten flour mixture and stir briskly with a wooden spoon to form a ball.

Place the gluten ball on a 12-inch (30 cm) square piece of cheesecloth or foil. Wrap it into a tight parcel; if using cheesecloth, it's probably a good idea to secure it with kitchen twine. Steam for 40 minutes, replenishing the water as needed.

Remove the ham from the steamer and let it cool briefly. If you won't be using it right away or if you have leftovers, wrap it tightly and store it in the refrigerator, where it will keep for up to 2 weeks.

 **ISLAND TIP**

For a tighter, firmer texture, bake the "ham" for 20 minutes at 400°F (200°C) after steaming it. As it bakes, baste it with a mixture of ¼ cup (62 ml) pineapple juice and two tablespoons maple syrup and stud it with a few whole cloves.

Lentil Roast

This is my spin on the classic vegetarian dish. The Bajan seasoning and molasses give this dish some bold new flavors. Serve it topped with Onion Gravy (page 35) and accompanied by a tossed salad.

1 slice toasted bread

1 cup (200 g) dried brown lentils, soaked overnight or quick-soaked (see Island Tip)

3½ cups (875 ml) water

½ cup (80 g) bulgur

1½ cups (375 ml) boiling water

2 tablespoons olive oil

1 large onion, chopped

1 carrot, grated

3 green onions, minced, or 2 tablespoons Bajan Seasoning (page 19)

¼ cup (50 g) fine bread crumbs

1 or 2 garlic cloves, pressed

¼ cup (40 g) nutritional yeast flakes

1 tablespoon cornstarch

1 teaspoon dried thyme

½ teaspoon mild paprika

½ teaspoon black pepper

Pinch of hot pepper flakes, optional

1 tablespoon unsulphured blackstrap molasses

Bragg Liquid Aminos or salt

GLAZE

¼ cup (62 ml) tomato sauce

Pinch of chili powder

½ teaspoon onion powder

Sprinkle of dried sage

Place the toast in a food processor and grind to medium-coarse crumbs. Put the lentils and 3½ cups (875 ml) of the water in a saucepan over medium-high heat. Bring to a boil, then turn the heat down to medium-low, cover, and cook for about 40 minutes, until soft. Drain thoroughly.

Meanwhile, combine the bulgur and 1½ cups (375 ml) of boiling water in a small saucepan over medium-low heat, cover, and cook for 15 to 18 minutes, until all of the water is absorbed.

Heat the olive oil in a small skillet over low heat. Add the onion, carrot, and green onions and sauté for about 10 to 15 minutes, until the vegetables are tender.

Preheat the oven to 350°F (180°C). Grease a standard loaf pan.

Put the sautéed vegetables, lentils, and fine bread crumbs in a food processor and pulse until well incorporated but not entirely smooth. The mixture should have a texture like stiff cake batter.

Scrape the mixture into a bowl. Add the bulgur, garlic, nutritional yeast, cornstarch, thyme, paprika, black pepper, pepper flakes, and molasses. Season with the Bragg Liquid Aminos to taste.

Spoon the mixture into the prepared pan and bake for about 50 minutes. Meanwhile, stir all of the glaze ingredients together. Brush the glaze on top of the loaf and sprinkle with the sage. Bake for 10 more minutes, until the sauce forms a slight crust over the roast.

Let the loaf cool before slicing, so that it will slice well without being mushy.

☀ ISLAND TIP

To quick-soak the lentils, add enough boiling water to cover by about 2 inches and let them sit for about 20 minutes.

Barbadian Pelau

Pelau is a flavorful rice dish, usually colored with browning. This pelau recipe is Barbadian-style. Do not confuse it with Trinidadian pelau, which uses pigeon peas and is cooked in coconut milk. Pigeon peas are optional in this recipe, but they will increase the nutritional value of the dish. Either way, it is a satisfying one-pot meal. I love it with Trinidadian Coconut Chutney (page 31) or Bajan Pepper Sauce (page 23).

1 cup (150 g) textured vegetable protein (TVP) chunks or faux chicken strips

1 tablespoon plus 1 teaspoon Bajan Seasoning (page 19) or Trinidadian Green Seasoning (page 22)

2 tablespoons olive oil

1 onion, finely chopped

1 carrot, diced into 1-inch (2.5 cm) cubes

3 garlic cloves, pressed

2 green onions, finely chopped

10 to 15 green beans, chopped in ½-inch (1.3 cm) pieces

½ cup (100 g) fresh, frozen, or canned pigeon peas, optional

1 tablespoon Caribbean Caramel (page 25) or browning

1½ teaspoons tomato paste

1 teaspoon Bajan Pepper Sauce (page 23)

3 cups (750 ml) water

1 tablespoon vegan Worcestershire sauce

1 tablespoon Bragg Liquid Aminos or soy sauce

1 tablespoon soy sauce

½ teaspoon Angostura bitters

1 teaspoon Madras curry powder

½ teaspoon mild paprika

3½ tablespoons ketchup

1½ cups (293 g) white basmati rice, rinsed

1 teaspoon minced thyme, or ½ teaspoon dried thyme

1 tablespoon vegan margarine

Salt and pepper

Pour just enough boiling water over the TVP to cover it. Let the TVP hydrate for 5 to 10 minutes. Pour off any excess water and coat the TVP with the Bajan Seasoning. Let stand for 20 minutes.

Heat the olive oil in a soup pot over medium heat. Add the onion, carrot, garlic, green onions, green beans, and optional pigeon peas and sauté for 5 minutes, until the vegetables begin to get tender. Stir in the seasoned TVP and Caribbean Caramel. Add the tomato paste, pepper sauce, and 1½ cups of the water. Add in the Worcestershire sauce, Bragg Liquid Aminos, soy sauce, bitters, curry powder, and paprika. Then, add the ketchup, rice, and thyme. Turn the heat down to medium-low, cover, and cook for about 13 minutes, until very thick and fragrant.

Add the remaining 1½ cups water. Cover and cook for about 25 minutes, until most of the liquid has been absorbed. Test the rice to ensure that it's tender. If not, add another ½ cup (125 ml) water and cook for about 5 more minutes.

Turn the heat down as low as possible, add the margarine, and fluff with a fork. Season with salt and pepper to taste. With the pot still on low heat, uncover the pot and let the rice dry out for 5 to 7 minutes. Fluff again and serve warm.

 **ISLAND TIP**

You could use 1 cup of chicken-style seitan instead of TVP. Feel free to substitute short-grain white rice, as it can withstand longer boiling than basmati. If you do, you need to decrease the amount of water to 2½ cups (625 ml).

White Sweet Potato Shepherd's Pie

SERVES 4

Give your old shepherd's pie topping a makeover by using white sweet potatoes instead of regular potatoes! Onion Gravy (page 35) is a good topping for this pie.

POTATO TOPPING

1 white sweet potato, chopped

1 tablespoon vegan margarine

3 cloves roasted garlic (see Island Tip), optional

⅓ cup (83 ml) coconut milk

Salt

FILLING

¾ cup (188 ml) boiling water

¾ cup (75 g) textured vegetable protein (TVP) granules

3 tablespoons Bajan Seasoning (page 19)

2 teaspoons olive oil

1 onion, chopped

1 shallot, minced

1 teaspoon chopped fresh thyme, or ¼ teaspoon dried

1 cup (250 ml) water

3 tablespoons nutritional yeast flakes

1 teaspoon mild paprika

1 teaspoon black pepper

1 teaspoon Madras curry powder

½ teaspoon ground cumin

¼ cup (62 ml) tomato sauce

1 tablespoon Bragg Liquid Aminos or soy sauce

1 tablespoon tomato paste

1 tablespoon American-style prepared mustard

1 teaspoon Bajan Pepper Sauce (page 23), optional

½ teaspoon Marmite or Vegemite

3 garlic cloves, pressed

Salt

Olive oil

Sprigs of fresh or dried rosemary

To make the potato topping, cook the sweet potatoes in boiling salted water for about 20 to 25 minutes, until just tender. Drain, add the margarine, optional garlic, and coconut milk, and mash until smooth. Season with salt to taste.

While the potatoes are cooking, make the filling. Pour the boiling water over the TVP, stir, and let stand for 5 to 10 minutes. If any liquid remains, drain it off. Add the Bajan Seasoning.

Heat the oil in a skillet over medium heat. Add the onion and sauté for about 3 minutes, until translucent. Add the TVP and sauté for 5 minutes, until slightly browned. Stir in the shallot, thyme, water, nutritional yeast, paprika, black pepper, curry powder, tomato sauce, Bragg Liquid Aminos, tomato paste, mustard, optional pepper sauce, and Marmite. Cook, stirring occasionally, for about 15 to 20 minutes.

Preheat the oven to 350°F (180°C). Grease an 8-inch (20 cm) square casserole.

Add the garlic to the TVP mixture and cook, stirring occasionally, for 10 minutes. Season with salt to taste.

Spread a very thin layer of mashed sweet potatoes in the bottom of the prepared pan. Add the TVP mixture and top with the remaining mashed sweet potato. Decorate with a drizzling of olive oil and the rosemary sprigs.

Bake for 20 minutes, then turn on the broiler and cook for 10 more minutes, until lightly browned, watching that it doesn't burn (set the broiler on low, if it has multiple settings).

 ISLAND TIP

You can substitute yams (not so-called yams that are really orange sweet potatoes) or regular potatoes if you wish. Shepherd's Pie is excellent with sweet peas in the filling. To roast the garlic, place one whole garlic on a piece of foil and drizzle with a little olive oil and a few rosemary leaves, wrap, and bake in a 350°F (180°C) oven for 30 minutes.

Vegan "Beef" Patties

Remember, in the Caribbean *patties* are pastries stuffed with various fillings. These patties are made with a flavored pastry dough and filled with a TVP preparation that is similar to ground beef. Serve these at your next picnic with some tossed salad.

PASTRY

3 cups (375 g) plus 2 tablespoons unbleached all-purpose flour

1 tablespoon salt

1½ tablespoons Madras curry powder

1½ tablespoons turmeric

1 cup (227 g) vegan margarine, plus more for brushing the pastry

⅔ cup (160 ml) ice-cold water

FILLING

1 cup boiling water

1 cup (100 g) textured vegetable protein (TVP) granules

2 tablespoons Jamaican Jerk Seasoning (page 20)

1½ teaspoons Marmite or Vegemite

2 tablespoons canola oil or another neutral-flavored oil

¾ onion, finely chopped

½ green bell pepper, finely chopped

4 garlic cloves, pressed

1 Scotch bonnet or habanero pepper, seeded and finely chopped

1 tablespoon Madras curry powder

¼ teaspoon black pepper

¼ teaspoon white pepper

½ teaspoon dried thyme

¼ teaspoon ground cumin

2 heaping tablespoons thick tomato sauce

⅓ cup (75 ml) water

½ teaspoon salt

3 tablespoons (43 g) margarine

3 tablespoons bread crumbs

To make the pastry, put the flour, salt, curry powder, and turmeric in a large bowl. Add the margarine and rub it into the flour with your fingertips or a pastry blender until the mixture resembles coarse crumbs. Slowly add the water, mixing into the dough with as little stirring as possible. If you wish, divide the dough into half to make it easier to work with. Wrap the dough in waxed paper and refrigerate for 1 hour.

Meanwhile, prepare the filling. Pour the boiling water over the TVP, stir, and cover. Let the TVP hydrate for 5 to 10 minutes. If any liquid remains, pour it off. Put the TVP in a bowl, add the jerk seasoning and Marmite, and mix well.

Heat the oil in a skillet over very low heat. Add the onion, bell pepper, and garlic and sauté for 7 minutes, until tender. Cover and cook for 4 minutes over low heat, until the onions have released some liquid. Stir in the TVP. Add the Scotch bonnet, curry powder, black pepper, white pepper, and thyme. Stir the tomato sauce into the water, then add it to the skillet, along with the salt, margarine, and bread crumbs. Cook, stirring occasionally, for 3 minutes. Taste and adjust the salt if necessary.

Cut the pastry dough into 12 equal pieces. Roll each piece out to a diameter of 4 inches (10 cm). The pastry should be fairly thin. Stack the disks with waxed paper between them and refrigerate for 20 to 30 minutes.

Preheat the oven to 400°F (200°C). Line a baking sheet with parchment paper.

Place a generous 1½ tablespoons of the filling on a disk of pastry. Fold the pastry in half to make a half-moon shape. Seal the edges by pressing them with the tines of a fork. Prick each patty a few times with a fork to help steam escape during cooking.

Put the patties on the lined baking sheet and bake for about 12 minutes. Remove from the oven, brush gently with a bit of melted margarine, then bake for about 12 more minutes, until the patties are cooked through. Serve warm or at room temperature.

 ISLAND TIP

Do not overfill the patties. During baking, this can cause excess steam to build up within the patties, and they may burst open. Even if they burst just a little, juices from the filling can make the finished pastry look unattractive.

Lentil Patties

Patties are a street food found all over the Caribbean. These stuffed pastries, usually made with meat or a mixture of vegetables, are seen as a portable high-protein meal. Lentil patties make an excellent packed lunch for vegans. You can also make them smaller and serve them as appetizers.

1 cup (250 ml) boiling water

½ cup (45 g) dried brown lentils

2 tablespoons olive oil

½ onion, finely chopped

2 large garlic cloves, minced

2 tablespoons finely chopped green bell pepper

¼ teaspoon minced Scotch bonnet or habanero pepper, optional

1 teaspoon ground cumin

1 tablespoon Madras curry powder

1 teaspoon white pepper

2 cups (500 ml) water

1 tablespoon tomato paste

1 tablespoon Bragg Liquid Aminos or soy sauce

1 teaspoon vegan Worcestershire sauce

½ teaspoon salt, or to taste

2 tablespoons bread crumbs

1 Basic Short Crust Pastry recipe (page 196), chilled

¼ teaspoon turmeric mixed with 1 tablespoon water, for brushing the pastry

Pour the boiling water over the lentils and let them soak for 20 to 30 minutes. Drain thoroughly.

Heat the oil in a skillet over medium heat. Add the onion, garlic, bell pepper, optional Scotch bonnet, lentils, cumin, curry powder, and white pepper. Sauté for about 4 minutes, until the onions are tender. Stir in 1 cup of the water and the tomato paste, Bragg Liquid Aminos, and Worcesterchire sauce. Turn the heat down to medium-low, cover, and cook for 15 minutes. Stir in another ½ cup of the water and the salt and continue to simmer, uncovered, for 5 minutes, stirring occasionally. Add the remaining ½ cup water and turn the heat down to low. Cook for about 10 more minutes, until the mixture starts to thicken. Add the bread crumbs and salt and cook, stirring constantly, until the mixture forms a thick brown paste. Remove from the heat and let cool to room temperature.

Preheat the oven to 400°F (200°C). Line a baking sheet with parchment paper.

Cut the pastry dough into 4 equal pieces. Gently and quickly roll each piece out to a diameter of 5¼ inches (13 cm). Put approxminately ¼ cup of the cooled lentil mixture in the middle of each, and fold the pastry in half to make a half-moon shape. Seal the edges by pressing them with the tines of a fork. Prick each patty a few times with a fork to help steam escape during cooking.

Place the patties on the lined baking sheet and brush them with the turmeric water. Put them in the refrigerator until the oven is fully preheated. Bake for 7 minutes, then lower the heat to 350°F (180°C) and bake for an additional 18 minutes, until golden brown. These are best cooled and eaten slightly above room temperature.

 **ISLAND TIP**

You might like to serve these with a glass of juice, as they are a little spicy. Do not overfill the patties. During baking, this can cause excess steam to build up within the patties, and they may burst open. Even if they burst just a little, juices from the filling can make the finished pastry look unattractive.

Trinidadian Doubles

Where can you find a vegan street food so widely available that if you miss one stall another is close by? Trinidad and Tobago, baby! You're probably wondering, "What are doubles, anyway?" Doubles are made up of two flat and fluffy fritters, called *bara*, that are stuffed with a hot chickpea stew and occasionally topped with chutney. This Trinidadian street food has made its way to Barbados and several other islands on a smaller scale. Doubles vendors don't use split pea flour in their bara, but I do, as it adds more nutritional value and gives the fritter a hearty bite.

BARA

1¼ teaspoons active dried yeast

1½ teaspoons brown sugar

1½ cups (375 ml) warm water (110°F to 115°F / 43°C to 46°C)

3 cups (375 g) unbleached all-purpose flour

½ cup (62 g) split pea flour or an additional ½ cup unbleached all-purpose flour

1½ teaspoons baking powder

¾ teaspoon salt

1 teaspoon Madras curry powder

1 teaspoon ground cumin

Canola oil

FILLING

3 tablespoons canola oil

1 onion, finely chopped or sliced into thin crescents

6 garlic cloves, pressed

Two 15.5-ounce (800 g) cans chickpeas or 3½ cups (765 g) cooked chickpeas

1 tablespoon Madras curry powder

1 tablespoon ground cumin

1 teaspoon black pepper

2 cups (500 ml) water

½ teaspoon turmeric

1½ teaspoons salt

1 teaspoon Bajan Pepper Sauce (page 23), optional

1 tablespoon finely chopped cilantro

1½ teaspoons chickpea flour

To make the bara, stir the yeast and sugar into the water and let stand for about 15 minutes, until the top is foamy. (If the yeast doesn't foam, it's dead or the water was too hot or too cool. You need to start over with fresh yeast.)

Put the flour, split pea flour, baking powder, salt, curry powder, and cumin in a bowl. Add the yeast mixture and stir until the dough comes together. It should be very soft; don't be tempted to add any additional flour. Put the dough in a bowl lightly greased with canola oil. Cover and let rise in a warm, draft-free place for about 2 hours, until doubled in size.

Meanwhile, make the filling. Heat the oil in a saucepan over medium heat. Add the onion and garlic and sauté for 1 minute. Stir in the chickpeas, curry powder, cumin, black pepper, water, turmeric, salt, optional pepper sauce, and cilantro. Turn the heat down to low and cook, stirring occasionally, for 15 minutes. Add the chickpea flour and cook, stirring occasionally, for 4 minutes, until the sauce thickens slightly.

Divide the dough into 24 pieces and form them into small balls; they will be very sticky so as you make them put them on a clean, greased flat surface.

Heat 1½ inches (4 cm) of oil over medium-high heat and test the oil after 5 minutes by dropping a piece of the dough into the oil. The oil is ready when the dough sizzles vigorously and browns quickly.

With oiled hands, stretch a dough ball (see photo insert, page 8.) Some holes may form in the dough as you stretch, and that is okay. Gently lower the bara into the hot oil, and, to help ensure you don't burn yourself, make sure that your two index fingers are the last fingers that leave the bara. Fry each bara using the 5-10-5 rule: 5 seconds on one side, 10 seconds on the other side, and 5 more seconds on the first side. Remove with tongs and drain. Oil your hands again, and continue until all of the bara are fried.

To assemble the doubles, cut twelve 7-inch (18 cm) squares of waxed paper. Place two bara on a piece of waxed paper, overlapping. Top with about 2 to 3 heaping tablespoons of filling. Bring the two sides of the paper together and wrap the double tightly, securing the wrapping by twisting the ends. To eat the doubles, peel back the paper.

☀ ISLAND TIP

I put my bara in a closed container when they are finished cooking. This makes them softer and more pliable. Green Mango Chutney (page 30) is excellent on doubles. Cucumber Chutney (page 32) is also nice.

Island Burgers

This is the burger I used to make for my university friends when they came over to study at my house. To me, an Island Burger is a burger with a big Caribbean influence. I recommend serving these patties on Salt Bread (page 48), with Pineapple Barbecue Sauce (page 38) or Sauce Chien (page 28) for condiments. Make some Spicy Baked Sweet Potato Wedges (page 148) to serve alongside. Do not forget the sugary Fried Plantains (page 161)—and a big appetite.

1 cup (250 ml) boiling water

1 cup (100 g) textured vegetable protein (TVP) granules

2 slices whole-grain bread, toasted

1 carrot, grated

4 green onions (green part only), finely chopped

1 tablespoon finely chopped fresh basil, or 1 teaspoon dried

1 tablespoon chopped mild chile peppers, such as Hungarian wax pepper, optional

2 large garlic cloves, pressed

½ Scotch bonnet or habanero pepper

1 to 2 tablespoons ketchup

1 tablespoon Bajan Seasoning (page 19)

1 tablespoon soy sauce

2 teaspoons vegan Worcestershire sauce

1 teaspoon Angostura bitters

1 teaspoon American-style prepared mustard

3 tablespoons unbleached all-purpose flour

2 tablespoons gluten flour, optional

2 tablespoons fine bread crumbs

1 tablespoon cornstarch

¼ teaspoon ground allspice

½ teaspoon mild paprika

½ teaspoon salt

Pour the boiling water over the TVP, stir, and cover. Let the TVP hydrate for 5 to 10 minutes. Gently squeeze out the excess water, but don't squeeze too hard or the final mixture will be too dry.

Put the toasted bread in a food processor and pulse to form coarse crumbs. Add the TVP, carrot, green onions, basil, optional mild chiles, garlic, and Scotch bonnet and pulse for a few seconds, until the mixture is chopped fairly fine.

Transfer the mixture to a bowl. Add the ketchup, Bajan Seasoning, soy sauce, Worcestershire sauce, bitters, mustard, flour, optional gluten flour, fine bread crumbs, cornstarch, allspice, paprika, and salt. Mix well. With floured hands, divide the mixture into 6 equal portions and shape into patties.

To cook the burgers, heat a bit of oil in a large skillet over medium heat. Fry the patties for about 4 minutes on each side, until cooked through in the middle. You can also bake them (see Island Tip).

 **ISLAND TIP**

You can bake the patties instead of frying. Just put them in a 350°F (180°C) oven for 20 to 22 minutes, turning once halfway during the cooking process.

If you haven't made any Pineapple Barbecue Sauce but want to use some on your burger, here's a quick shortcut: Puree 2 rings of canned pineapple and 2 tablespoons of pineapple juice, then stir in 1 cup of store-bought barbecue sauce.

To freeze the patties, layer them between sheets of waxed paper and place in a freezer bag. Thaw them before cooking. If the thawed patties are too wet and crumbly, add a little flour and bread crumbs and reshape them before cooking.

Jug-Jug

This is my take on jug-jug, a Barbadian Christmas pudding usually made from left-over pigeon peas and ham. It is thought that the original recipe for jug-jug was derived from the Scottish dish haggis, which may have been brought to Barbados by Scottish indentured servants. The dish was transformed by local ingredients, using pigeon peas as the base of the dish and millet as a thickening agent. This dish is a great high-protein entrée for the winter season. Jug-jug can also be served as a side or eaten as a dip, with crackers, carrot sticks, and celery, and I think it is the perfect filling for stuffed tomatoes.

½ cup (125 ml) boiling water

½ cup (45 g) textured vegetable protein (TVP) granules

1 tablespoon Bajan Seasoning (page 19) or Trinidadian Green Seasoning (page 22)

2 tablespoons olive oil

1 onion, finely chopped

¼ cup (50 g) Everyday Vegan "Ham" (page 100) or smoky vegan sausage, finely chopped

½ teaspoon liquid hickory smoke

1 cup (170 g) fresh, frozen, canned, or cooked pigeon peas

½ teaspoon minced Scotch bonnet or habanero pepper

1 green onion, minced

1 teaspoon chopped fresh thyme, or ¼ teaspoon dried

1½ cups (375 ml) water

⅓ cup (79 ml) vegetable stock

1 tablespoon vegan Worcestershire sauce

1 tablespoon plus 1 teaspoon millet flour

Salt to taste

Vegan margarine

Pour the boiling water over the TVP, stir, and cover. Let the TVP hydrate for 5 to 10 minutes. Don't drain the TVP after hydrating. Stir in the Bajan Seasoning.

Heat the olive oil in a saucepan over medium heat. Add the TVP with its seasoning, along with the onion, vegan ham, and liquid smoke. Turn the heat down to medium-low and sauté for 5 minutes, until the onion is translucent. Stir in the pigeon peas, Scotch bonnet, green onion, thyme, water, stock, and Worcestershire. Cover and cook for 20 minutes.

Drain the jug-jug, reserving the liquid, and put the pea mixture in a food processor. Process until fairly smooth. If the reserved liquid amounts to less than ½ cup (125 ml), top it up with water.

Return the liquid to the saucepan and place it over medium heat. Stir in the millet flour. It will absorb the water and start to swell. Once it does, return the blended pea mixture to the pot and mix well. Turn the heat down to low and cook, stirring occasionally, for 5 minutes, until the mixture looks like a thick paste. Season with salt to taste, and serve with a bit of margarine on top.

Vegan Steamed Pudding and Souse 📷

This is my favorite recipe in the book, but I admit that it's an acquired taste. You really have to be a little adventurous to try this one. It's based on a traditional meat dish served in Barbados for brunch and lunch on Saturdays, which undoubtedly originated from the British dish black pudding, since Barbados was ruled by the British until 1966. In Barbados, the recipe was adapted to use the vegetables available at the time: sweet potatoes. Traditionally, the pudding was stuffed into sausage casings, but over the last ten years I have noticed that more people tend to go for the pudding cooked in a baking pan or steamed in a bowl. For the faux chicken in the souse component of this dish, I recommend Morningstar Farms Meal Starters Chik'n Strips. I find that it absorbs more of the flavor than seitan does. However, you can use any meat substitute you like, or even a combination. You can substitute sweet potatoes for the breadfruit in the pickle, but it will taste different and the dish will not be as authentic. The pickle and souse are served cold, but the steamed pudding is usually warm. The meat version of this dish is sold in select shops and restaurants all over Barbados, and some people sell it out of their homes or just make it on the weekend for the family.

PUDDING

2½ cups (400 g) finely grated white sweet potato

1 medium-large onion, minced

4 green onions, finely chopped

1 Scotch bonnet or habanero pepper, seeded and minced

2 teaspoons minced fresh thyme, or ½ teaspoon dried

¼ cup (63 ml) water

3 tablespoons vegan margarine

1 tablespoon Caribbean Caramel (page 25) or browning

¼ cup (50 g) brown sugar

¼ teaspoon salt

1 tablespoon seasoning salt

1 teaspoon ground cloves

PICKLED BREADFRUIT

1 medium-large cucumber, peeled and finely chopped

1 onion, minced or grated

2 tablespoons fresh lime juice

1 Scotch bonnet or habanero pepper, seeded and minced

3 tablespoons finely chopped parsley

1 teaspoon chopped fresh thyme, optional

1 teaspoon chopped dill, optional

1 teaspoon salt

½ cup (125 ml) ice-cold water

½ teaspoon seasoning salt

¼ breadfruit, cooked and chopped into cubes, or one 19-ounce (538 g) can of breadfruit in brine

SOUSE

1 cup (250 ml) water

Bouquet garni (see page 5) made with 1 small chive and a few sprigs each of thyme and marjoram

1 Scotch bonnet or habanero pepper

½ teaspoon seasoning salt

Juice of ½ lime

1 cup (200 g) cubed faux chicken

Preheat the oven to 350°F (180°C). Grease a 7½ x 3¾-inch (19 x 10 cm) loaf pan.

To make the pudding, combine all of the ingredients and stir until well combined. Transfer to the greased loaf pan and cover with foil. Bake for about 35 minutes, then remove from the oven, stir the uncooked middle into the cooked sides, and take this opportunity to taste the pudding. Adjust for sugar and salt if necessary, then return the pudding to the oven and bake for about 35 more minutes, until the pudding is brown, soft, and scoopable.

Combine the cucumber, onion, lime juice, Scotch bonnet, parsley, optional thyme and dill, salt, seasoning salt, and water in a bowl and stir until well combined. Let the mixture stand for about 20 minutes at room temperature; this allows some of the water to seep out of the cucumber, adding some liquid to the sauce. Add the bread-fruit and let it soak for 20 to 30 minutes, to absorb the flavors. Taste and adjust the seasonings; you can add more salt, pepper, or lime juice if you like.

While the breadfruit is soaking up the flavors, make the souse. Bring the water to a simmer. Add the bouquet garni, Scotch bonnet, seasoning salt, and lime juice. Add the faux chicken, adjust the heat to maintain a gentle boil, and cook for 7 minutes. Remove from the heat, cover, and let stand for 20 minutes to infuse the faux chicken with flavor. Remove the bouquet garni and discard.

To assemble the dish, put some of the pudding on a plate. Serve it warm by the spoon-ful, or let it cool and then cut into squares. Serve some of the pickle and souse along-side. Cover everything with some of the liquid from the pickle before serving.

Cou-Cou and Tofish

Tofish paired with Cou-Cou and Creole Sauce makes this vegan version of Barbados' national dish, Cou-Cou and Flying Fish. The tofu I like to use in this recipe is the Leasa brand in firm. It is slightly cheaper than other brands and has the best texture for this recipe. Nasoya brand in firm and extra-firm works well, too, but it will give the Tofish a slightly different texture, and it will not look like the the photograph in the book (see photo insert, page 6). Be prepared for a full-flavored piece of tofu with a mild spicy kick.

TOFISH

1 cup (250 ml) water

2 tablespoons olive oil

2 teaspoons Bajan Seasoning (page 19)

2 sheets nori, snipped into small pieces with scissors

3 green onions, finely chopped

1 teaspoon finely chopped Scotch bonnet or habanero pepper

1 teaspoon salt

1 pound (454 g) firm tofu, sliced into 4 slabs

TOFISH SAUCE

15 basil leaves

1½ tablespoons chopped cilantro

3 mild red chile peppers, or 1 Scotch bonnet or habanero pepper, seeded

½ onion, chopped

1 garlic clove

1½ tablespoons olive oil

½ cup (125 ml) tofish marinade, with nori

2 tablespoons vegan margarine

½ teaspoon coarsely ground black pepper

1 recipe Creole Sauce (page 30)

1 recipe Cou-Cou (page 122, see Island Tip)

To make the tofish, whisk the water, olive oil, Bajan Seasoning, nori, green onions, Scotch bonnet, and salt together until thoroughly combined. Pour the marinade in a shallow dish. Gently place the tofu in the marinade and let it stand for at least 1 hour and up to 3 hours. The longer it marinates, the more flavorful the results.

About 15 minutes before you are ready to serve, make the sauce. Put the basil, cilantro, mild chiles, onion, and garlic in a food processor. Pour in the ½ cup of marinade and process until fairly smooth, but do not overprocess, as the sauce should have some texture.

To cook the tofish, heat the olive oil in a large nonstick skillet over high heat. Gently tranfer the tofish to the skillet, and sear for about 3 to 4 minutes on each side, turning periodically if needed, until browned.

Turn the heat down to medium. Pour the tofish sauce over the tofish, ensuring that it is coated generously. Add the margarine to the pan and, as it melts, coat the tofish with this as well. Season the tofish with black pepper and cook for 5 additional minutes, turning periodically.

Prepare the Creole Sauce, then prepare the Cou-Cou.

TO SERVE

To assemble the dish, grease a plastic bowl with margarine, add about ½ cup of cou-cou to the bowl for one serving, and shake the bowl until the cou-cou is coated with margarine and has formed into a smooth ball. Turn the cou-cou out onto a plate, make an indentation in the top of the ball, spoon Creole Sauce over, top with Tofish, and finish with more Creole Sauce. Serve hot.

 ISLAND TIP

Always make Cou-Cou last. Prepare the tofish and the Creole Sauce first, then make the cou-cou and assemble the dish while the cou-cou is hot. Cou-cou hardens as it cools and this hardening is irreversible.

Cou-Cou

The definition of *cou-cou* varies. It can mean the carbohydrate component of the national dish of Barbados, made with cornmeal and cooked with okra. It can also mean a food that's mashed to create a puree or a paste, as in the Breadfruit Cou-Cou recipe (page 151) in the side dish chapter. Other islands have a version of cornmeal cou-cou without the okra, and Grenada and other islands cook cou-cou with coconut milk in a method like an oil down (see page 140). In the Island Territory of Sint Maarten, in the Netherlands Antilles, a version of cou-cou without okra is made; it is called *fungi* (pronounced "fun-gee"). Cou-cou–making techniques vary from household to household. Many Bajans swear by the cold water technique, in which the cornmeal is soaked in cold water before it's added to the boiling water. Be prepared for an arm workout, because you need to constantly stir the cou-cou throughout the process, taking some little breaks in between. I find it easier to make cou-cou by what I call the streaming method which is used for polenta. The cornmeal is slowly poured into the boiling water while stirring constantly with a cou-cou stick (see photo), or a strong wooden spoon or spatula. Cou-cou is not a stand-alone dish and should be served in Cou-Cou and Tofish (page 120).

> **4¼ cups (1 liter) water**
> **2 teaspoons salt**
> **12 to 15 small okra pods, sliced or ⅔ cups frozen**
> **1½ cups (160 g) fine cornmeal**
> **2 teaspoons Bajan Seasoning (page 19)**

Bring the water and salt to a boil in a large, heavy saucepan. Add the okra and boil for 6 minutes. Pour off half of the slimy okra water, reserving it to add back in later. Don't worry if you lose a few of the okra slices when you pour the water off.

Return the pot to the stove over medium heat. Pour in the cornmeal slowly, in a steady stream, whisking continuously to prevent lumps, and adding a little of the reserved okra water back in. You need to work quickly here, as the mixture will start to lump up.

Turn the heat down to medium-low. Stir in a little more of the okra water with the cou-cou stick or wooden spoon. Stir the cou-cou vigorously for 3 minutes until the cou-cou mixture is lump free, or close to being lump free.

Slowly add back in all of the remaining okra water, along with any errant okra slices, stirring and pressing the thick mixture continuously. Turn the heat down to low. When all of the lumps are gone, cook the cou-cou over medium-low heat for 5 to 7 minutes. Add the Bajan Seasoning and incorporate it thoroughly into the cou-cou. Reduce the heat to low. Take the pot of cou-cou from the stove and place it on a tea towel and stir vigorously for 2 minutes. At this stage the cou-cou mixture will be difficult to stir, but you must stir through the thickness. Put the pot back on the stove and leave the cou-cou to cook. You should hear the cou-cou puffing from the steam. The cou-cou should take 25 to 30 minutes to cook from the time it is added to the okra water. The cou-cou is done when the cornmeal tastes well cooked and the mixture is smooth, without any visible cornmeal grains.

Serve immediately with tofish and Creole Sauce (see page 121 for serving instructions). Do not allow the cou-cou to cool.

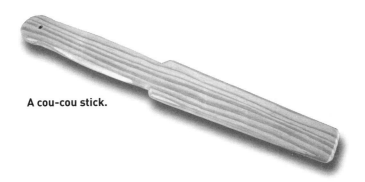

A cou-cou stick.

Bajan Macaroni Pie
with Tofu Cheddar

SERVES 6

You may be thinking, "Mac and cheese in the Caribbean?" But in Barbados, macaroni pie is made daily in restaurants and on Sundays and holidays in the home. Bajan macaroni pie is orange due to the mixture of American-style mustard and ketchup, and flavorful due to the Bajan Seasoning, onions, and mixed herbs. After baking, it is cooled a bit and then sliced. If you've been disappointed by other vegan mac and cheese recipes, try this one. I promise that it is the most authentic macaroni pie you will find and that it will satisfy all your cheese cravings. If you make this for your next potluck or for a group of skeptical omnivores, they will not believe that it doesn't contain dairy or even vegan cheese.

TOFU CHEDDAR
5 ounces (150 g) medium-firm tofu
½ teaspoon cornstarch
Small pinch of turmeric
2 tablespoons unsweetened nondairy milk
½ teaspoon salt

ROUX
⅓ cup (76 g) vegan margarine
⅓ cup (42 g) plus 1 tablespoon unbleached all-purpose flour
¾ cup (188 ml) unsweetened nondairy milk
1 heaping tablespoon American-style prepared mustard
2 tablespoons nutritional yeast flakes
Salt

13 ounces (375 g) uncooked macaroni noodles
3 tablespoons ketchup, or more to taste
1 medium-small onion, finely grated
2 large garlic cloves, pressed
1 heaping tablespoon Bajan Seasoning (page 19)
1½ teaspoons American-style prepared mustard
½ teaspoon Bajan Pepper Sauce (page 23), optional
1 teaspoon mild paprika
1 teaspoon black pepper
1 teaspoon white pepper
1½ teaspoons chopped parsley
1½ teaspoons chopped fresh thyme, or ½ teaspoon dried
Salt

2 tablespoons bread crumbs
2 teaspoons vegan margarine

To make the tofu cheddar, put all of the ingredients in a food processor and pulse until medium smooth. Tiny pieces of tofu should still be visible.

To make the roux, heat the margarine in a small saucepan over medium heat. While whisking continuously, first sprinkle in the flour, then slowly pour in the nondairy milk. Cook, whisking from time to time, for about 3 minutes, until thickened. Remove from the heat. Stir in the mustard and nutritional yeast. Salt to taste.

Preheat the oven to 350°F (180°C). Grease an 8-inch (20 cm) square or round baking pan.

Cook the macaroni in a generous amount of boiling salted water until somewhere between soft and al dente. Drain well and transfer to a large bowl.

Gently stir in the tofu cheddar and roux. Add the ketchup, onion, garlic, Bajan Seasoning, mustard, optional pepper sauce, paprika, black pepper, white pepper, parsley, and thyme. Season with salt to taste.

Spread the mixture evenly in the prepared pan. Sprinkle the bread crumbs on top, then dot with the margarine. Bake for 1 hour, until the pie forms a nice crust.

Cool for about 30 minutes. Cut into 3-inch (8 cm) squares or wedges and serve warm.

 ISLAND TIP

Barbadian macaroni pie is made with long macaroni that is broken into 2-inch pieces before cooking. If you cannot get this kind of macaroni, use elbows or precut macaroni. This pie can be as spicy or sweet as you like. Many Barbadians add a little more ketchup, and some add more pepper. The good thing about this recipe is that you can taste it and adjust the saltiness, heat, and sweetness to suit yourself. If you want a cheesy, bubbly crust, make a second batch of roux and stir in a little ketchup. Pour this on top of the pie and sprinkle with bread crumbs. Feel free to use whole wheat or multigrain macaroni. Or try jazzing up this already flavorful pie with cubes of Everyday Vegan "Ham" (page 100).

Lasagna

It is said that Barbados has some of the biggest pasta lovers in the Caribbean. Some Bajans eat pasta nearly every day. If it isn't macaroni pie, it's lasagna. The most common type of lasagna is a Bolognese, which I've recreated here with a vegan twist. The TVP or seitan is cooked up in a sauce; I recommend using a roasted garlic marinara sauce for more flavor. For a more attractive red color, be sure to include the optional tomato paste. This dish is perfect for a casual dinner party.

9 ounces (255 g) lasagna noodles, cooked and drained

SAUCE
2 cups boiling water

2 cups (200 g) textured vegetable protein (TVP) granules

2 tablespoons Bajan Seasoning (page 19)

3 tablespoons olive oil

1 medium-large onion, chopped

4 garlic cloves, pressed

½ cup (100 g) Vegan Everyday "Ham" (page 100), chopped, optional

10 to 15 leaves basil, chopped

3 cups (750 ml) prepared marinara sauce

1 tablespoon vegan Worcestershire sauce

1 tablespoon tomato paste, optional

1 teaspoon Bajan Pepper Sauce (page 23)

1 teaspoon black pepper

Salt

TOFU CHEEZE
15 ounces (425 g) firm or medium-firm tofu

2 green onions, chopped

1 garlic clove, chopped

1 tablespoon cornstarch

2 teaspoons dried oregano

Salt and pepper

ROUX
½ cup (113 g) vegan margarine

1 cup (125 g) unbleached all-purpose flour

2 cups (500 ml) unsweetened nondairy milk

3 tablespoons nutritional yeast flakes

½ teaspoon white pepper

½ teaspoon ground nutmeg

½ teaspoon American-style prepared mustard

Salt and pepper

To make the sauce, pour the boiling water over the TVP, stir, and cover. Let the TVP hydrate for 5 to 10 minutes. If any liquid remains, drain it off. Stir in the Bajan Seasoning.

Heat the olive oil in a saucepan over medium heat. Add the TVP, onion, garlic, optional vegan ham, and basil and sauté for 5 minutes, until slightly browned. Stir in the marinara, Worcesterchire sauce, optional tomato paste, pepper sauce, and black pepper. Season with salt to taste. Cook, stirring occasionally, for 7 minutes, until sauce thickens slightly.

To make the tofu cheeze, combine the tofu, green onions, garlic, cornstarch, and oregano, in a food processor and process until fairly smooth. Season with salt and pepper to taste.

To make the roux, heat the margarine in a small saucepan over medium-low heat. Sprinkle in flour, whisking continuously and cook for 30 seconds. Slowly pour in the nondairy milk, still whisking continuously to prevent any lumps from forming. Cook, whisking from time to time, for about 5 minutes, until thickened. Stir in the nutritional yeast, white pepper, nutmeg, and mustard. Season with salt and pepper to taste.

Mix the roux and tofu cheeze together.

Preheat the oven to 350°F (180°C).

Assemble the lasagna in a 9 x 13-inch (23 x 33 cm) baking pan. Spread a little of the sauce in the bottom of the pan. Top with a layer of ⅓ of the noodles, then spread an even layer of ⅓ of the roux and tofu cheeze mixture. Repeat additional layers of sauce, then noodles, then roux. You should have three layers at the end. Your top layer can be either sauce or the mixture of roux and tofu cheeze. Bake for 45 minutes, until nicely browned. Cool for 25 minutes before cutting.

☀ ISLAND TIP

 *If you don't* like TVP, try this recipe using minced seitan or cooked red lentils instead.

Jerk Pizza with Sweet Potato Crust 📷

This pizza is saucy and flavorful and if you give this to anyone they will be so wrapped up in the crust and the toppings that cheese will be the last thing on their mind.

CRUST

7 ounces (200 g) white-fleshed sweet potato, chopped

1 teaspoon active dry yeast

1 teaspoon sugar

½ cup (125 ml) lukewarm water (110°F to 115°F / 43°C to 46°C)

2 tablespoons olive oil

1 teaspoon dried thyme

2 cups (250 g) unbleached all-purpose flour

1 teaspoon onion powder

1 teaspoon salt

SAUCE

One 8-ounce can prepared tomato sauce or pizza sauce

1 teaspoon molasses

1 teaspoon Jamaican Jerk Seasoning (page 20)

1 to 2 teaspoons brown sugar

½ teaspoon seasoning salt

¼ teaspoon cornstarch

¼ teaspoon Madras curry powder

⅛ teaspoon cayenne pepper

½ Scotch bonnet or habanero pepper, chopped, optional

TOPPINGS

2 tablespoons olive oil, plus more as needed

2 or 3 Jerk "Sausages" (page 98), sliced into ½-inch (1.3 cm) rounds

1 ripe plantain, sliced into ½-inch (1.3 cm) rounds

¾ cup (150 g) Morningstar Farms Meal Starters Chik'n Strips
   or frozen and defrosted tofu (see Island Tip)

1 tablespoon Jamaican Jerk Seasoning (page 20)

1 tablespoon soy sauce

¼ teaspoon salt

1 small eggplant, peeled and cut into short, thin strips

1 garlic clove, minced

1 medium onion, cut into rings or crescents

3 green onions, finely chopped

A few slices of green and red bell pepper

A sprinkle vegan cheese, optional

2 tablespoons cornmeal

1 teaspoon olive oil

1 teaspoon dried thyme

To make the crust, cook the potatoes in boiling salted water for 20 to 25 minutes, until tender. While the potatoes are cooking, stir the yeast and sugar into the ½ cup of water and let stand about 15 minutes, until the top is foamy. (If the yeast doesn't foam, it's dead or the water was too hot or cool. Start over with fresh yeast.)

Drain the potatoes and put them in a large bowl. Add the olive oil and thyme, and mash until smooth. Add the yeast mixture, flour, onion powder, and salt and using your hands knead well until the dough comes together.

Knead the dough in the bowl for 10 minutes, until it becomes fairly smooth and pliable. You may need to add a bit more flour to get the proper consistency. Lightly oil the bowl with olive oil, cover, and set in a warm, draft-free place for 1 to 1½ hours.

Punch the dough down and knead it for 5 minutes, until fairly smooth.

To make the sauce, put all of the ingredients in a saucepan over medium-high heat and stir until well combined. Bring to a simmer, then cover and turn off the heat.

Preheat the oven to 350°F (180°C).

To prepare the toppings, heat the oil in a skillet over medium-high heat. Add the sausage and cook for about 4 minutes, turning periodically until lightly browned. Transfer to a plate, lined with paper towels if you'd like to absorb some of the oil. Put the plantains in the skillet and cook for about 2 minutes on each side, until lightly browned. Transfer the plantains to the plate with the sausage. Marinate the Chik'n Strips in the jerk seasoning and soy sauce. Add a little olive oil in the same pan and brown the strips slightly over medium heat. Take out and set aside. Sprinkle the salt over the eggplant. Add a little olive oil to the skillet and turn the heat down to medium. Add the eggplant and sauté for 4 minutes, until tender. Add the garlic and sauté for 2 minutes, until cooked. Turn off the heat.

Sprinkle the 2 tablespoons of cornmeal on a pizza pan. Roll the dough out to a diameter of 16 inches (40 cm) for a thin crust, or 12 inches (30 cm) for a regular crust. Put the crust on the pan and brush it with the 1 teaspoon olive oil. Spread the sauce over the top, then add the toppings in any order, but saving the vegan cheese for the top.

Bake for 25 minutes, then sprinkle the thyme over the top. Bake for about 5 more minutes, until the crust is golden.

☀ ISLAND TIP

If you are not a fan of Morningstar Farms Meal Starters Chik'n Strips you can freeze a block of tofu, thaw it completely and squeeze out the excess water. From there you can chop it up and marinate it with the seasonings in the recipe. This method changes the texture of the tofu, giving it a chewier bite. This pizza can be made with whole wheat flour mixed with 2 tablespoons of vital wheat gluten. For the "pepper mouths" reading this, you can sprinkle additional minced Scotch bonnets on the pizza—if you dare!

SIDE
DISHES

IN THE CARIBBEAN, side dishes are quite varied. Common staples like rice, pasta, and potatoes are the norm, but we also make good use of local and traditional produce, which we call ground provisions—things like yams, breadfruit, and plantains. You can find most of the ground provisions in these recipes in ethnic markets. If you can't find them locally, feel free to make substitutions. All of these side dishes are flavorful—so much so that some of them tend to upstage the main course!

Spanish Rice

I first was introduced to this dish in my food and nutrition class at secondary school. It was the one rice dish most of the girls in that class actually made at home. I was a bit dubious about its authenticity because the Spanish rice my father made when I was a child was red with tomatoes and made with pieces of meat. When I went vegan, I thought I had to give up this dish, because the original version relied heavily relied on New Zealand cheddar cheese, but trusty tofu and herbs and spices did the trick. Because it includes tofu, it's a balanced meal on its own. For even more protein, serve it alongside a bean stew.

> 1 cup (200 g) uncooked white basmati rice
> 2½ cups (625 ml) water
> 2 tablespoons plus 1 teaspoon vegan margarine
> 1 medium-large onion, chopped
> ½ green bell pepper, minced
> 2 tomatoes, chopped or thinly sliced
> 1 tablespoon Madras curry powder
> 7 ounces (200 g) medium or firm tofu
> 2 tablespoons unsweetened nondairy milk
> 1 teaspoon salt
> ½ teaspoon turmeric
> ½ teaspoon cornstarch
> 2 tablespoons ketchup
> 1 teaspoon American-style prepared mustard
> 2 tablespoons chopped parsley
> Salt and pepper
> 3 tablespoons fine bread crumbs

Combine the rice and water in a small saucepan over high heat. Bring to a boil, then lower the heat, cover, and simmer for about 15 minutes, until all of the water is absorbed.

Meanwhile, place an oven rack near the top of the oven and preheat the broiler (set to low, if your broiler has such a setting).

Heat the 2 tablespoons of margarine in a large skillet over medium-low heat. Add the onion, bell pepper, tomatoes, and curry powder and sauté for 6 minutes, until the mixture starts to get saucy.

Put the tofu, nondairy milk, salt, turmeric, and cornstarch in a blender or food processor and process until smooth. Stir the mixture into the sautéed vegetables along with the rice, ketchup, mustard, and parsley. Season with salt and pepper.

Grease an 8-inch (20 cm) square baking pan. Transfer the mixture into the prepared pan, dot the top with the 1 teaspoon margarine, and sprinkle with the bread crumbs.

Broil the casserole for about 20 minutes, until the rice is cooked through and the top is lightly browned. Cool for 20 minutes before serving.

Creole Rice

In the Caribbean, Creole rice usually means white basmati rice cooked with salt. It can also be a red-colored rice flavored with spices and a bit of peanut butter, as in this recipe. If your peanut butter is very thick, heat it in the microwave before adding it to the dish so it will mix in better. You can use dried Louisiana-style Creole seasoning in this recipe, as it is quite similar to the type used in the French West Indies. Sautéeing the annatto seeds in the oil is an optional step, but it's worth doing as it gives the rice a nice red color.

1 teaspoon vegetable oil

¼ teaspoon annatto seeds, optional

1 onion, finely chopped

2 garlic cloves, pressed

1 carrot, finely chopped

½ celery stalk, minced

1 cup (195 g) white basmati rice, rinsed

2½ cups (625 ml) water

⅓ cup (80 ml) tomato sauce

1 teaspoon tomato paste

1 tablespoon peanut butter

1 tablespoon Creole seasoning

1 tablespoon chopped parsley

1 teaspoon chopped fresh thyme, or ¼ teaspoon dried

1 teaspoon salt

1 Scotch bonnet pepper

Heat the oil in a saucepan over medium-low heat. If using the annatto seeds, add them and cook for a few minutes, until the oil is infused with a red color, then spoon them out or strain the oil. Add the onion and garlic to the oil and sauté over medium-low heat for about 5 minutes, until the onion is slightly translucent. Add the carrot, celery, and rice, turn the heat up to medium, and sauté for 5 minutes.

Stir in the water, tomato sauce, tomato paste, peanut butter, Creole seasoning, parsley, thyme, and salt. Gently stir in the Scotch bonnet, being very careful not to rupture it, as this would make the rice overly spicy. Turn the heat down to medium-low, cover, and cook for about 20 minutes, until all of the liquid has been absorbed. If the rice still isn't tender, add another ⅓ cup (79 ml) water and cook for about 5 more minutes, until rice is tender.

Turn the heat down as low as possible and fluff the rice with a fork, again being very careful not to rupture the pepper. Cook, uncovered, for 3 to 5 minutes, until the rice has dried out. Serve hot.

 **ISLAND TIP**

In this recipe, the hot pepper is used for flavor, not heat. The flavor from the Scotch bonnet is really good and this method of cooking with an entire pepper extracts flavor without so much heat. Just be sure to pay attention when fluffing the rice, as the prongs of the fork can rupture the pepper!

Spinach Rice

This rice can be made with spinach, bok choy, or any green leafy vegetable that cooks up soft. In the Caribbean, we typically use either spinach or bok choy to make this dish. This goes well with Chickpea Curry (page 88).

1 tablespoon olive oil
1 onion, chopped
3 ounces (84 g) chopped spinach
1½ cups (293 g) white basmati rice, rinsed
3 cups (750 ml) water
1 teaspoon salt

Heat the olive oil in a saucepan over medium heat. Add the onion and sauté for about 3 minutes, until translucent. Try to avoid burning the onion, as this would make the rice look dirty. Stir in the spinach and turn the heat down to medium-low. Add the rice, then stir in the water and salt. Cover, and simmer for about 25 minutes, until most of the water has been absorbed.

Turn the heat down as low as possible, fluff the rice with a fork, and cook, uncovered for a few more minutes. The rice should be dry, not sticky, when it's finished. Serve hot.

Pigeon Pea Rice

Many people associate Caribbean food with rice and peas, and they are right. This classic Caribbean rice dish is made with a variety of peas or beans and served as a side dish. On many islands, people tend to use pigeon peas, also known as gungo peas. Note that dried and canned pigeon peas have slightly different flavors.

2 tablespoons olive oil

½ onion, sliced into crescents

1 cup (200 g) fresh, frozen, or canned pigeon peas

2 garlic cloves, sliced

1½ teaspoons Bajan Seasoning (page 19)

Bouquet garni (page 5) made with a few sprigs each of thyme and marjoram, and 2 green onions

Pinch of mild paprika

Pinch of black pepper

1 cup (210 g) white short-grain rice, rinsed

3½ cups (875 ml) water

1 Scotch bonnet or habanero pepper

1 teaspoon adobo seasoning

1 teaspoon onion powder

½ to 1 teaspoon salt

2 garlic cloves, pressed

Heat the oil in a saucepan over medium heat. Add the onion, peas, sliced garlic, Bajan Seasoning, and bouquet garni and sauté for about 5 minutes, until onions are tender. (This process is called "doving the peas.") Add the paprika and black pepper, then stir in the rice, water, Scotch bonnet, adobo seasoning, onion powder, and salt. Lower the heat, cover, and simmer for 20 to 25 minutes or until all the water has evaporated and the rice is cooked dry.

Add the 2 cloves of pressed garlic and cook for about 5 more minutes, until all of the water has been absorbed. Discard the bouquet garni. Taste and adjust the salt if necessary.

ISLAND TIP

For the bouquet garni, there is no need to bundle it in cheesecloth as you may be accustomed to doing. This bouquet garni has a dual purpose of flavoring the rice and decorating it with flecks of thyme.

Curried Rice

This rice dish is an excellent side dish, but it is even better with a partner in crime, such as Onion Gravy (page 35) or Creole Sauce (page 36). The onion provides a nice sweet balance to the curry.

> **2 tablespoons olive oil**
> **1 tablespoon Madras curry powder**
> **½ onion, minced**
> **1 cup (195 g) white basmati rice, rinsed**
> **2 cups (500 ml) water**
> **1 teaspoon salt**
> **1 teaspoon turmeric**
> **1 teaspoon onion powder**
> **½ teaspoon adobo seasoning**
> **⅛ teaspoon cayenne pepper, optional**

Heat the oil in a saucepan over medium heat. Add the curry powder and cook, stirring, for 30 seconds. Add the onion and sauté for about 5 minutes, until translucent. Stir in the rice and sauté the rice for 3 minutes. Stir in the water, salt, turmeric, onion powder, adobo seasoning, and optional cayenne. Cover and cook over medium-low heat for about 23 minutes, until all of the water has been absorbed.

Turn the heat down as low as possible, fluff the rice with a fork, and cook, uncovered, for 3 to 5 minutes, until the rice has dried out a bit.

 ISLAND TIP

Feel free to add fresh or frozen sweet peas, for color contrast and nutritional value. Just stir them in when you add the rice.

Coconut Rice

Coconut rice is a real crowd-pleaser. This rice dish is bold and colorful from the herbs and spices and the coconut milk almost gives it a buttery flavor that will keep your guests going back for more. This method of cooking the rice in coconut milk, called an oil down, is similar to the method for Vegan Grenadian Oil Down (page 154). For an Ital meal, leave out the salt and pair this rice with Mixed Bean Stew (page 90).

1 tablespoon coconut oil or canola oil

1 onion, minced

3 green onions, minced

6 garlic cloves, 4 whole and 2 pressed

1 celery stalk, finely chopped

2 tablespoons chopped parsley

1 tablespoon chopped fresh thyme, or ¾ teaspoon dried

2¼ cups (563 ml) coconut milk

1½ cups (293 g) white basmati rice

1½ teaspoons salt

1 teaspoon black pepper

½ teaspoon mild paprika

¼ teaspoon turmeric

¼ teaspoon ground allspice

1 to 2 tablespoons minced mixed herbs (such as marjoram, thyme, or basil), green onions, or a combination

¼ cup minced mild chile peppers, such as Hungarian wax peppers

Heat the coconut oil in a saucepan over medium-low heat. Add the onion, green onions, garlic, celery, parsley, and thyme, and sauté for 5 minutes, until the vegetables are tender. Stir in the coconut milk, rice, salt, black pepper, paprika, turmeric, allspice, minced mixed herbs, and mild chiles. Lower the heat, cover, and simmer for about 25 minutes, until all of the water has been absorbed.

Turn the heat down as low as possible, fluff the rice with a fork, and cook, uncovered, until the rice has dried out. Serve hot.

Creole Spaghetti

If you need a quick and easy dish after work or school, this one-pot meal of spaghetti cooked in Caribbean-style sauce may fit the bill. There is no fixed recipe for making Creole spaghetti; the ingredients vary from island to island. In Saint Martin in the French West Indies, open-air food establishments sell Creole spaghetti. This recipe is similar to the version they make.

7 ounces (200 g) spaghetti

½ cup (150 g) chopped chicken-style seitan or other meat substitute

1 tablespoon Bajan Seasoning (page 19) or Trinidadian Green Seasoning (page 22)

1½ teaspoons adobo seasoning

1 tablespoon canola oil

1 onion, minced

4 garlic cloves, pressed

1 red bell pepper, chopped

1 green bell pepper, chopped

1 tablespoon minced mild chile peppers, such as Hungarian wax peppers, optional

1½ cups (375 ml) water

4 tablespoons ketchup

2 tablespoons vegan Worcestershire sauce

2 teaspoons Angostura bitters, optional

1 teaspoon onion powder

½ teaspoon white pepper

2 teaspoons chopped parsley

Salt and black pepper

Cook the spaghetti in a generous amount of boiling salted water until just tender.

While the spaghetti is cooking, season seitan or other meat substitute with Bajan seasoning and adobo seasoning. Set aside.

Heat the oil in a large saucepan over medium heat. Add the onion, garlic, bell peppers, and optional mild chiles and sauté for 2½ minutes, until the vegetables are tender. Turn the heat down to medium-low, stir in the seitan, then stir in the water, ketchup, Worcestershire sauce, optional bitters, onion powder, and white pepper.

Cook, stirring occasionally, for about 5 minutes, until the sauce has thickened and reduced slightly.

Drain the spaghetti and add to the sauce. Stir gently until well mixed, then add the parsley and season with salt and pepper to taste. Serve hot.

 **ISLAND TIP**

I recommend whole wheat or multigrain spaghetti for this dish. In place of the seitan, you could use hydrated TVP chunks or cubes of a commercial meat substitute like Morningstar Farms Meal Starters Chik'n Strips or hydrated Butler Soy Curls. If you don't want a sweet pasta sauce, use tomato sauce instead of ketchup in this dish. And feel free to add any vegetable you like to this dish. Most vegetables can be added along with the onions. You may need to increase the cooking time a bit so that the vegetables are tender to your liking.

Vegetable Chow Mein

After emancipation, many Chinese indentured servants in the Caribbean stayed on these islands. Many opened small village grocery shops, and often they made chow mein at home and sold it in their shops. West Indian cooks made the dish their own by using sauces with Caribbean flavors and, on some islands, using browning to color the sauce. This stir-fry does not taste like takeout, but like something extraordinary.

2 tablespoons canola oil

½ onion, sliced into thin crescents

3 garlic cloves, minced

½ bell pepper, any color, cut into thin strips or diced small

15 to 20 green beans, chopped

1 medium carrot, diced small

1 cup (150 g) chopped chicken-style seitan, tofu, or faux chicken strips

2 tablespoons soy sauce, or more to taste

1 tablespoon Bajan Seasoning (page 19), Jamaican Jerk Seasoning (page 20), or Trinidadian Green Seasoning (page 22)

1 teaspoon Caribbean Caramel (page 25) or browning, optional

One 1-inch (2.5 cm) piece ginger, cut into thin strips

½ cup (125 ml) water

½ teaspoon black pepper

½ teaspoon white pepper

½ teaspoon Madras curry powder

¼ teaspoon mild paprika

1 tablespoon tomato paste

1 teaspoon American-style prepared mustard

7 ounces (200 g) egg-free chow mein noodles

3 ounces (84 g) spinach, thinly shredded

2 small garlic cloves, pressed

1 teaspoon Bajan Pepper Sauce (page 23) or Asian hot chili sauce

Salt, optional

Heat 1 tablespoon of the oil in a large skillet over medium heat. Add the onion, 2 of the minced garlic cloves, and the bell pepper, green beans, and carrot. Turn the heat down to very low and sauté for 15 to 20 minutes.

Meanwhile, put the seitan in a saucepan and mix it with the soy sauce, Bajan Seasoning, and optional Caribbean Caramel. Stir in the remaining minced garlic clove, ginger, and water and place over low heat. Stir in the black pepper, white pepper, curry powder, paprika, tomato paste, and mustard and simmer for about 25 minutes, until the liquid has reduced to a fairly thick and slightly sticky sauce.

Cook the noodles in a generous amount of boiling salted water until just tender.

Add the remaining 1 tablespoon oil to the vegetables. Add the spinach and cook gently for just a minute or two, until the spinach is wilted.

Drain the noodles well. Add them to the pan of vegetables and stir gently. Add the seitan with its sauce, along with the 2 cloves of pressed garlic, and the chili sauce. Season with soy sauce to taste, then season with salt if you like. Serve hot.

 ISLAND TIP

This can be made without any meat substitute. You can play around with adding peas or your favorite vegetables to make this dish even more unique.

Dal Puri Roti

Roti is a type of Indian flat bread, but on some of the islands, *roti* refers to a dish of curry wrapped in roti bread. In this book, I use the term *roti* in both ways. This roti bread, or skin, as we call it, can be used to envelop Sautéed Okra (page 166), Sautéed Spinach (page 157), Curried Potatoes and Pumpkin (page 150), Chickpea Curry (page 88), Curried TVP Stew (page 87), and other curry dishes. Making filled roti may seem daunting, but they are actually easy to make, and once you've made them a few times you'll get the hang of it. Be sure to follow the step-by-step photos on page 10 of the photo insert. Do not worry about making them perfectly circular. I never aim for perfect circles. Just have fun with the process. I will say that making great roti skins takes patience; do not try to make this when you are in a hurry. If roti is something you like and you want to make it often, invest in a tawa (see page 12, and photo insert page 10) or at least a crepe pan or cast-iron skillet.

FILLING

⅔ cup (100 g) dried yellow split peas, soaked overnight or quick-soaked (see Island Tip)

½ Scotch bonnet or habanero pepper, seeded and minced

2 tablespoons chopped cilantro

4 garlic cloves, pressed

1 tablespoon ground cumin

¾ teaspoon salt, or to taste

DOUGH

3½ cups (438 g) unbleached all-purpose flour

1½ teaspoons salt

2 teaspoons baking powder

½ teaspoon turmeric, optional

3½ tablespoons vegan margarine

¼ cup (62 ml) canola oil

1 cup (250 ml) warm water

To make the filling, drain and rinse the peas, then cook them in boiling water for 8 minutes, until semi-cooked. Drain thoroughly, then cool for 30 minutes. Dry the peas on a tea towel to remove any excess water.

Put the peas in a food processor, along with the Scotch bonnet, cilantro, garlic, cumin, and salt. Pulse until the mixture looks like fine couscous.

To make the dough, put the flour, salt, baking powder, and optional turmeric in a large bowl and stir to combine. Add the margarine and rub it into the flour with your fingertips or a pastry blender until the mixture resembles fine bread crumbs. Add the canola oil and water and mix with a fork to incorporate the water into the flour until the dough comes together.

Knead the dough in the bowl for about 7 minutes, until very smooth. Brush the dough with oil and set aside. Put the dough in a lightly oiled bowl in a warm, draft-free place, and let rest for 30 minutes to 1 hour.

Oil a plate or small baking tray. Cut the dough into 6 equal pieces. Working on a lightly floured surface, roll each piece out to a diameter of about 5 inches (13 cm), rolling the edges thinner and leaving the center thick, but not too thick, as the dough needs to be flexible enough to shape around the filling (see photo insert, page 10).

Hold a piece of dough in one hand to form a cup shape. Fill the cup with 2 to 3 heaping tablespoons of filling. Pinch the edges together to secure the filling, then form the dough into a clean ball. Flatten slightly and set aside on the oiled plate. Let the filled roti balls rest in a covered plate for 30 minutes.

Working on a lightly floured surface, roll each ball out until it is about 12 to 14 inches (30 to 36 cm) in diameter, taking into account the size of your pan. You want the rolled rotis to be just shy of the size of the cooking surface. The rolled roti skin should be thin, like a flour tortilla. If the dough bursts and exposes the filling during rolling, you can try to save the skin by folding it again and rerolling.

Put a griddle or tawa over medium heat and brush with a thin layer of oil. Place a skin on the griddle. Cook for 30 seconds, then turn and cook for 12 seconds on the other side, brushing the edges of the roti with oil as it cooks. Turn off the heat. You can leave the roti on the tawa for a few more seconds as the residual heat in the tawa will finish cooking the roti.

Layer the cooked rotis with waxed paper between them. Serve warm.

☀ ISLAND TIP

 To quick-soak the split peas, add enough boiling water to cover by about 2 inches (5 cm) and let them sit for about 20 minutes. Note that the cooked skins freeze well and can be thawed in a matter of minutes. You can steam them or cook them on a griddle for a few seconds to reheat them.

Buss-Up-Shut Roti

You may know buss-up-shut by its Indian name: *paratha*. It is a plain roti that is cooked and then slapped, hit with sticks, or clapped by hand to give it a flaky texture. The term *buss-up-shut* comes out of Trinidadian dialect and means "busted-up shirt." The name is fitting, as the process of slapping the roti after cooking gives it the appearance of a shredded shirt. As with Dal Puri Roti (page 145), in the final rolling you want to make these about the size of your cooking surface, so a larger griddle or tawa means a thinner roti. Serve these with Yellow Split Pea Dal (page 93) or any curry you like.

> **4 cups (500 g) unbleached all-purpose flour**
> **1 teaspoon baking powder**
> **½ teaspoon salt**
> **1 teaspoon light brown sugar**
> **1½ tablespoons oil**
> **1½ cups (375 ml) water, or more as needed**

Mix the flour, baking powder, salt, sugar, and oil in a large bowl. Make a well in the middle of the flour mixture and add the water. Bring the mixture together with your fingertips and knead in the bowl for about 7 minutes, until soft and elastic. You may need to add an extra tablespoon of water to get the dough to come together properly. Put the dough in a lightly oiled bowl in a warm, draft-free place, cover, and let rest for 1 to 2 hours

Knead the dough for about 2 minutes, until smooth. Cut the dough into 6 equal pieces. Working on a lightly floured surface, roll each piece out to a diameter of at least 5 inches (12 cm). Cut the dough from the center to one side only, as if you are cutting a radius into the circle (see photo insert, page 11). Roll the dough from the cut center to form a cone. Using your index finger, push the tip of the cone into the dough. This will form a dough disk that looks like a cinnamon roll. Repeat with remaining pieces. Put the dough disks back into the oiled bowl in a warm, draft-free place, cover, and let rest and rise for 45 minutes.

Working on a floured surface, roll each disk out to just about the size of the cooking surface. Heat a griddle or tawa over medium-high heat and brush with a thin layer of oil. Place a roti on the griddle and cook for 30 to 45 seconds, brushing the edges of the roti with oil. Turn and cook for 1 minute on the second side. Remove the cooked roti and, using two wooden spoons or a spatula, beat it for about 30 seconds, until the surface is ruptured and flaky. Serve warm.

Spicy Baked Sweet Potato Wedges

In the Caribbean, sweet potatoes chips or fries are usually made with white sweet potatoes. Because of their low moisture content, white sweet potatoes hold their shape well, and because they have a mild flavor, they take on the flavor of the seasoning nicely. For a real taste sensation, dip them in Pineapple Barbecue Sauce (33). In this recipe, the sweet potatoes are baked, so they're lower in fat but still delicious. If you like, you can fry the potatoes instead, and then toss them with the spices.

1 pound, 6 ounces (600 g) white-fleshed sweet potatoes
2 teaspoons onion powder
1 teaspoon salt
1 teaspoon Creole seasoning
½ teaspoon cayenne pepper
½ teaspoon black pepper
½ teaspoon dried thyme
½ teaspoon Madras curry powder
½ teaspoon chili powder
⅛ teaspoon ground cinnamon
⅛ teaspoon mild paprika
⅓ cup (83 ml) olive oil

Preheat the oven to 400°F (200°C).

Peel the sweet potato and cut it into long strips that resemble French fries. Pat the sweet potatoes dry.

Mix the onion powder, salt, Creole seasoning, cayenne, black pepper, thyme, curry powder, chili powder, cinnamon, and paprika together in a medium bowl. Add the olive oil and stir until well combined. Put the sweet potatoes in the bowl and toss with the seasoned oil.

Spread the sweet potatoes and seasoned oil on a baking sheet (there is no need to separately grease the baking sheet). Bake for 25 minutes, turning twice during the cooking process. The cooked fries should be tender when pricked with the tines of a fork.

Classic Barbadian Sweet Potato Pie 📷

This sweet potato dish is traditionally served on Sundays or on special occasions. The topping is stunning: pineapple slices and cherries—you have to love that. Feel free to double or triple the recipe, but I prefer this pie in small quantities, served with a bit of Onion Gravy (page 35). Ordinarily, this pie is baked in a baking pan and then cut into squares for serving, but my version calls for making individual pies.

1 pound, 6 ounces (600 g) white- or yellow-fleshed sweet potatoes, coarsely chopped

2 tablespoons vegan margarine

½ cup (125 ml) pineapple juice

1 teaspoon ground cinnamon or cassia

Salt

2 pineapple slices

2 cherries

Cook the sweet potatoes in boiling salted water until tender.

Preheat the oven to 350°F (180°C). Grease two 5-inch (13 cm) ramekins.

Drain the sweet potatoes, add the margarine, pineapple juice, and cinnamon, and mash until smooth. Season with salt to taste.

Transfer to the greased ramekins. Top each pie with a pineapple slice and a cherry. Bake for 20 to 25 minutes, until lightly browned around the sides. Serve warm.

Curried Potatoes and Pumpkin

SERVES 4 AS A SIDE DISH, OR 6 IF USED AS A ROTI FILLING

This sweet and spicy curry makes a perfect filling for the roti in Dal Puri Roti (page 145) or Buss-Up-Shut Roti (page 147). If using this curry as a filling for roti (see photo insert, page 10), it should be hot when you are assembling your roti.

2 tablespoons olive oil

2 tablespoons Colombo or Madras curry powder

1½ teaspoons ground cumin

½ teaspoon garam masala

1 onion, chopped

3 cups (750 ml) water

1 teaspoon salt, or to taste

2½ cups (600 g) diced potatoes, cut into 1½-inch (4 cm) cubes

1½ cups (400 g) diced calabaza squash, butternut squash, or other winter squash, cut into 1½-inch (4 cm) cubes

1½ teaspoons American-style prepared mustard

1½ teaspoons tomato paste

½ teaspoon Bajan Pepper Sauce (page 23), or ⅛ to ¼ teaspoon cayenne pepper

1 teaspoon black pepper

1 teaspoon mild paprika

1 teaspoon turmeric

3 to 4 garlic cloves, pressed

Heat the oil in a soup pot over medium heat. Add the curry powder, cumin, and garam masala and sauté for 30 seconds. Add the onion and stir to coat with spice mixture. Turn the heat down to medium-low. Stir in the water, salt, potatoes, and squash and cook for 10 minutes.

Gently stir in the mustard, tomato paste, pepper sauce, pepper, paprika, and turmeric and cook for about 25 minutes or, until the vegetables are tender. Add the garlic and cook for 10 minutes, until the liquid has reduced to a slightly thick sauce. Serve hot.

Breadfruit Cou-Cou

This creamy, buttery mash of breadfruit is usually served as part of a weekday lunch in Barbados. I suggest serving it topped with Creole Sauce, alongside Tofish (page 120).

½ **breadfruit**

⅓ **cup (70 g) vegan margarine**

2 **green onions, minced**

⅛ **teaspoon liquid smoke, optional**

½ **teaspoon salt, optional**

Cut the breadfruit into quarters, peel it, and remove the heart. Chop the flesh into large chunks. Cook the breadfruit in boiling water for about 20 to 25 minutes, until tender but still firm.

Drain the breadfruit, add the margarine, green onions, and optional liquid smoke and salt, and mash until smooth. This isn't like mashing potatoes; it will feel as if you're mashing glue or some type of dough. Grease a bowl, transfer the mixture to the bowl, and roll it around to form a ball. Make a well in the center of the cou-cou. You can ladle suitable sauces like Creole Sauce (page 36) and Onion Gravy (page 35) into the well.

 ISLAND TIP

Traditionally, this dish is cooked with a piece of salted pork, which is why I included liquid smoke in my version. You can leave it out if you prefer. You can also make this dish using 19 ounces (538 g) of canned breadfruit. Just gently reheat the canned breadfruit to soften it before mashing. Because canned breadfruit is packed in brine, there's no need to include the salt called for in the recipe.

Boil and Fry

This is a popular way of preparing root vegetables in Guyana. The vegetables are first boiled or steamed, and then sautéed with herbs and other aromatic ingredients. For a nice meal, pair it with Eggplant, Hearts of Palm, and Spinach Stew (page 153) and a slab of Tofish (page 120).

11 ounces (300 g) yam, cassava, or breadfruit, diced into 1½-inch (4 cm) cubes

1 green or half-ripe plantain

3 tablespoons olive oil or canola oil

½ onion, chopped

¾ cup (188 ml) coarsely chopped tomato

2 garlic cloves, minced

2 mild chile peppers, such as Hungarian wax peppers, minced, optional

¼ cup minced mixed herbs (such as parsley, basil, thyme, or marjoram), green onions, or a combination

Salt and pepper

Boil the yams in salted water until tender. (If using cassava, remember that it contains a toxic compound, so it's important to cook it fully.)

Meanwhile, steam the plantain in its skin until tender; you can test it by piercing it with a fork.

Heat the olive oil in a large skillet over medium-low heat. Add the onion, tomato, garlic, optional mild chiles, and mixed herbs and sauté for 4 minutes, until vegetables are tender. Peel and slice the plantain, then add it to the skillet. Gently stir in the yams and sauté for 5 to 7 minutes, until well-coated with the herbs and vegetables. Season with salt and pepper to taste.

Eggplant, Hearts of Palm, and Spinach Stew

This stew goes well with Boil and Fry (page 152), other cooked root vegetables, or any rice dish. The nori gives the dish a slight seaweed flavor. If that doesn't appeal to you, leave it out.

- **7 ounces (200 g) eggplant**
- **1 teaspoon salt, plus more to taste**
- **4 ounces (120 g) hearts of palm, coarsely chopped**
- **1 nori sheet, toasted and crumbled (see page 9), optional**
- **1 tablespoon Bajan Seasoning (page 19) or Trinidadian Green Seasoning (page 22)**
- **½ teaspoon Madras curry powder**
- **½ teaspoon black pepper**
- **2 tablespoons chopped green onion**
- **½ teaspoon mild paprika**
- **1 teaspoon chopped fresh thyme, or ¼ teaspoon dried**
- **½ Scotch bonnet or habanero pepper, seeded and minced**
- **1 garlic clove, minced**
- **1 tablespoon vegan margarine or olive oil**
- **1 cup (85 g) chopped spinach, optional**
- **½ cup (125 ml) water**
- **⅓ cup (79 ml) tomato sauce**
- **1 tablespoon ketchup**

Peel and cut the eggplant into medium-size strips or medium cubes. Sprinkle the eggplant with the 1 teaspoon salt and let it sit for 20 minutes to draw out any bitterness. Squeeze out the eggplant and rinse it lightly.

Place eggplant in a bowl and add hearts of palm, optional nori, Bajan Seasoning, curry powder, black pepper, green onion, paprika, thyme, Scotch bonnet, and garlic. Heat the margarine over low heat and add vegetable mixture and optional spinach. Sauté for 5 minutes until the vegetables are slightly browned. Stir in the water and tomato sauce, raise the heat to medium-low, and cook for 10 minutes, until the eggplant is cooked through. Season with salt to taste, and add more black pepper if you like. Serve hot.

Vegan Grenadian Oil Down

This recipe is influenced by Grenada's national dish, the oil down, which is root vegetables cooked in seasoned coconut milk with salted pork or meat until most of the coconut milk is absorbed in the vegetables, leaving a liquid that is mostly coconut oil. Oil down is a community food that is enjoyed with friends and family members and sometimes made outdoors. The vegetable of choice is cassava, but you can also use breadfruit. Traditional oil down is not vegan, as the dish is started off with salted pork, but you can approximate the flavor with some liquid smoke or a few pieces of Everyday Vegan "Ham."

1 tablespoon vegan margarine

½ onion, thinly sliced

3 garlic cloves, minced

1 tablespoon chopped mild chile peppers, such as Hungarian wax peppers

1 celery stalk, including leaves, chopped

½ cup (100 g) Everyday Vegan "Ham," chopped (page 100), optional

2 teaspoons chopped fresh thyme, or ½ teaspoon dried

12 ounces (350 g) cassava or breadfruit, diced into 2-inch (5 cm) cubes

2 cups (500 ml) coconut milk

3 ounces (84 g) spinach, shredded

1 teaspoon salt

½ teaspoon ground allspice

½ teaspoon turmeric

Heat the margarine in a large saucepan over medium-low heat. Add the onion, garlic, mild chiles, celery, optional vegan ham, and thyme and sauté for 4 minutes, until the vegetables are tender and ham starts to brown a little. Stir in the cassava, coconut milk, spinach, salt, allspice, and turmeric. Cover partway and cook for 50 minutes, until the cassava is tender and the oil has settled out. Pour the oil off if you like. Serve hot.

 ISLAND TIP

For a version that is lower in fat, you can use 1 cup of regular coconut milk and 1 cup of light. This makes a nice accompaniment to Bajan "Beef" Stew (page 85).

Creole Ratatouille

This dish is the French Caribbean's version of the popular French recipe. In Guadeloupe, they tend to grow a lot of cucumbers, hence cucumbers are a component of this dish. The difference between this version and regular ratatouille is the cucumbers, the christophene (chayote), and the hot peppers.

9 ounces (250 g) eggplant, coarsely chopped

1 teaspoon salt, plus more to taste

2 tablespoons olive oil

1 medium-large onion, coarsely chopped

5 garlic cloves, minced

1 tablespoon brown sugar

1 large cucumber, coarsely chopped

2 zucchinis, coarsely chopped

1 green bell pepper, coarsely chopped

1 red bell pepper, coarsely chopped

1 christophene (chayote), peeled, seed removed, and coarsely chopped

1 celery stalk, including leaves, chopped

½ teaspoon finely chopped Scotch bonnet or habanero pepper

1 cup (220 g) tomatoes, chopped

3 green onions, minced

1½ cups (375 ml) water

2 tablespoons tomato paste

1 teaspoon black pepper

¼ cup finely chopped parsley

1 teaspoon dried thyme

Sprinkle the eggplant with 1 teaspoon of the salt and let it sit for 10 minutes to draw out any bitterness. Gently rinse off the salt.

Meanwhile, heat the oil in a large, deep skillet or soup pot over medium heat. Add the onion, garlic, and brown sugar, and sauté for 2 minutes. Stir in the eggplant, cucumber, zucchini, bell peppers, christophene, celery, Scotch bonnet, tomatoes, green onions, water, and tomato paste. Cover and cook for about 25 minutes, until the vegetables are almost tender.

Stir in the black pepper, parsley, and thyme, and season with salt to taste. Cover and cook for 15 to 20 minutes, until all of the vegetables are well cooked. Serve hot.

ISLAND TIP

If you like your ratatouille thick, like I do, after cooking leave the dish at room temperature, covered, for about 1½ hours to thicken the sauce. Reheat when you are ready to serve.

Sautéed Spinach

This is my go-to easy recipe for sautéed spinach. This dish works well with dals or as a filling for the roti in Dal Puri Roti (page 145) or Buss-Up-Shut Roti (page 147).

¼ cup (57 g) vegan margarine
1 onion, minced
6 ounces (168 g) spinach, finely chopped
½ Scotch bonnet or habanero pepper, minced
2 teaspoons white pepper
½ teaspoon Madras curry powder
½ teaspoon ground cumin
½ teaspoon garam masala
½ cup (125 ml) water
Salt and black pepper

Heat the margarine in a large saucepan over medium heat. Add the onion and spinach and sauté for 4 minutes, until onions are translucent. Add the Scotch bonnet, white pepper, curry powder, cumin, garam masala, and water and cook for about 5 minutes, until the spinach is wilted and most of the water has evaporated. Season with salt and black pepper to taste and serve hot.

Warm Green Banana and Squash Stir-Fry

SERVES 4

This dish is a mixture of vegetables seasoned and cooked mildly. I chose green banana for this recipe is because it holds its shape well after cooking. If you can't find green bananas, you can substitute white or yellow sweet potatoes.

5 green bananas

1 teaspoon salt

1 butternut squash, cut into short, thin crescents

½ zucchini, coarsely chopped

1 tablespoon olive oil

1 onion, coarsely chopped

1 garlic clove, minced

1 large green bell pepper, coarsely chopped

4 green onions, chopped, or 1 tablespoon Trinidadian Green Seasoning (page 22)

½ cup (125 ml) water

1 large tomato, coarsely chopped

½ Scotch bonnet or habanero pepper, minced, or ¼ teaspoon hot pepper flakes

1 tablespoon finely chopped parsley

1 tablespoon Bragg Liquid Aminos or soy sauce

1 teaspoon black pepper

1 teaspoon ground cumin

Peel the bananas (see page 12), then boil them in salted water for about 25 minutes, until just tender when pricked with a fork. Drain and slice into rounds 2 inches (5 cm) thick.

Meanwhile, sprinkle the salt over the squash and zucchini and let stand for 10 minutes. Lightly rinse the squash.

Heat the oil in a large saucepan over medium-low heat. Add the onion, garlic, bell pepper, and green onions and sauté for 5 minutes, until vegetables are slightly tender. Add the squash and zucchini and sauté for 5 minutes. Gently stir in the cooked banana. Pour in ¼ cup (62 ml) of the water along the side of the pan, cover, and let the vegetables steam for about 15 minutes.

Gently stir in the tomato, Scotch bonnet, parsley, Bragg Liquid Aminos, black pepper, and cumin. Pour in the remaining ¼ cup water along the side of the pan. Cover and cook for about 25 minutes, until all of the water has evaporated and the squash is tender. Serve warm.

Mashed Green Bananas

Mashing green bananas in coconut milk results in a very flavorful dish that is almost cheesy—and addictive and filling. This dish is excellent topped with Creole Sauce (page 36) or Onion Gravy (page 35), or served alongside Creole Red Bean Stew (page 95).

10 green bananas
1 cup coconut milk
¼ to ½ onion, grated
1 garlic clove, pressed
1½ teaspoons adobo seasoning
1 teaspoon onion powder
½ teaspoon black pepper
Salt to taste

Peel the bananas (see page 12), then boil them in salted water for about 25 minutes, until tender when pricked with a fork. As they cook, their color should go from white to light brown or gray.

Drain the bananas and put them in a bowl. Add the coconut milk, onion, garlic, adobo seasoning, onion powder, and pepper. Mash the banana well, but it need not be completely smooth. The finished texture should be like a stiff, thick cake batter; you can leave in some chunks for more texture if you like. Taste and adjust the salt if necessary.

Fried Plantains

A good ripe plantain is sweet and flavorful. Plantains sold in the United States usually come from Mexico, though if you are lucky you may find some from the Caribbean in ethnic markets. I am not saying that everything in the Caribbean tastes better, but I find the plantains from this region taste sweeter than the Mexican variety. Caribbean plantains have a bright yellow skin, like bananas, and the skin blackens as they become riper. The Mexican variety has a dark yellow color, and the darkening tends to be in spots, not lines. Everyone fries plantains differently. I tend to cut them lengthwise or sometimes in wedges. Plantains are best fried in a neutral-flavored oil such as canola.

2 ripe plantains
¼ cup canola oil or another neutral-flavored oil

Peel the plantains and cut them into lengthwise slices. Heat the oil in a large skillet over medium heat. When the oil is hot, fry the plantains, turning them a time or two, for about 5 minutes, until golden brown or slightly darker. Drain on paper towels and serve warm.

 **ISLAND TIP**

If you serve these with a spicy dish, it is better to use very sweet, ripe plantains to complement the spicy flavor. In the Caribbean, fried plantains are very popular for breakfast alongside scrambled eggs. Try pairing one or two slices of fried plantain with your tofu scramble.

Steamed Plantains with Sauce Chien

Who said you have to fry plantains all the time? Sweet plantains are also good when boiled in the skin. If you carefully remove the skin after steaming, the plantain will still be intact. Prepared this way, they can be eaten with vegan margarine, Creole Sauce (page 36), or Onion Gravy (page 35), but I think Sauce Chien is tastiest.

> **4 ripe plantains**
> **2 teaspoons vegan margarine**
> **1 cup (250 ml) Sauce Chien (page 28)**

Trim off the ends of the plantains, then steam them in their skins for about 25 minutes, until tender.

Cut an incision down the length of the plantains. Dot the margarine on the plantains, then drizzle the Sauce Chien into the incision. Serve warm in the skin.

ISLAND TIP

If you only have half-ripe plantains, it is better to peel them before steaming. See page 12 for how to peel green plantains.

Okra in Sofrito Sauce

In this side dish, okra is cooked in a sofrito-type sauce, characterized by onion, garlic, bell pepper, and tomato. This dish makes a nice accompaniment to a veggie burger, or serve it with hot white rice.

2 tablespoons olive oil

24 okra pods, sliced ¼- to ½-inch (6 to 13 mm) thick

1 onion, chopped

4 garlic cloves, minced

5 tomatoes, chopped

6 tablespoons chopped green bell pepper or mild green chile peppers

¼ Scotch bonnet or habanero pepper, seeded and minced

½ cup chopped smoky vegan sausage

½ teaspoon liquid smoke

1 cup (250 ml) water

One 16-ounce (454 g) can regular tomato sauce, preferably Spanish-style

2 tablespoons Bragg Liquid Aminos or soy sauce

2 tablespoons chopped parsley

2 teaspoons chopped fresh thyme, or ¼ teaspoon dried

½ teaspoon white pepper

1 teaspoon salt, or to taste

Heat the oil in a saucepan over medium heat. Add the okra and sauté for 3 minutes, until lightly browned. Remove half of the okra and set aside. Add the onion, garlic, tomatoes, bell pepper, Scotch bonnet, vegan sausage, and liquid smoke. Sauté for 2 minutes, then turn down the heat to low and sauté for 2 more minutes. Stir in the water, tomato sauce, Bragg Liquid Aminos, parsley, thyme, white pepper, salt, and the remaining okra. Cook for 10 minutes. Taste and adjust the salt if necessary. Serve hot.

☀ ISLAND TIP

For this recipe to really pop, it's best to use a Spanish-style tomato sauce. Goya is the brand I tend to use. Spanish-style tomato sauce is slightly more acidic than regular tomato sauce, and also contains different spices.

When selecting okra, make sure it's firm, but you don't want it too hard, or it will be tough and fibrous. Okra doesn't have a long shelf life, so use it as soon as possible after purchase. Slicing the okra somewhat thick, as in this recipe, guarantees that it will still have some crunch once it's cooked.

Okra Slush

This is just what the name says: a slush of okra. As a side dish, it's best with rice and a curry. It can also be served as a soup, in which case you could blend it if you like.

> **4¼ to 5¼ cups (1 to 1.25 liters) water**
> **40 to 50 fresh okra pods, sliced into ½-inch (1.3 cm) rounds**
> **1 onion, finely chopped**
> **3 garlic cloves, pressed**
> **1 tomato, chopped**
> **1 small piece Scotch bonnet or habanero pepper**
> **1½ teaspoons salt**
> **¼ teaspoon celery salt**
> **¼ teaspoon dried thyme**
> **1 heaping tablespoon Trinidadian Green Seasoning (page 22)**
> **A few chunks of Everyday Vegan "Ham" (page 100), optional**
> **Lime wedges**

Bring the water to a boil in a soup pot. Add the okra, onion, garlic, tomato, Scotch bonnet, salt, celery salt, thyme, green seasoning, and optional vegan ham. Cook, uncovered, over medium-low heat for 35 to 40 minutes stirring occasionally, until the okra is very soft.

Taste and add more salt if you like. Serve with wedges of lime, to squeeze over the dish.

Sautéed Okra

This way of serving okra is different from the typical, more moist preparations that you may be accustomed to. This dish can be used as a filling for Dal Puri Roti (page 145) or Buss-Up-Shut Roti (page 147), or as an accompaniment to rice.

¼ cup olive oil
1 Scotch bonnet or habanero pepper, minced
4 to 6 garlic cloves, minced
50 okra pods, sliced
1 teaspoon ground cumin
Salt and black pepper

Heat the oil in a skillet over medium heat. Add the Scotch bonnet, garlic, and okra and sauté for about 5 minutes, until the okra browns. Stir in the cumin and season with salt and pepper to taste. Turn the heat down to medium-low and sauté for 3 minutes, until the okra is cooked through. Serve warm.

7

CARIBBEAN
TEA PARTY

IN THE CARIBBEAN, *tea* can mean a variety of beverages: not just caffeinated tea, but hot chocolate, fruit teas, noncaffeinated tisanes, and herbal tea, which sometimes is called "bush tea" in the region. When I was a little girl, my mother would offer me Milo or Ovaltine—whichever I was fond of at the time. As I got older, I moved on to peppermint and ginger and basil teas. The teas in this section are all noncaffeinated tisanes.

I will not go so far as to say that in the former British colonies we do not have teatime anymore. In the Caribbean there are still a large number of people who have tea in the middle of the day.

That said, tea is typically a component of supper, usually consumed with a dry cake or biscuit. In this short chapter, I share with you a few teas and accompaniments that I make for myself or that my mother made for me when I was growing up.

Rock Cakes

Like their name suggests, these cakes are hard like a rock. They are somewhat similar to scones but vary as they are made using the creaming method, while scones are made by rubbing the fat into the flour. Rock cakes are sold in bakeries and, on some islands, in rum shops. They are especially nice with Basil Tea (page 180).

½ cup (100 g) light brown sugar or granulated sugar

½ cup (113 g) vegetable shortening

1 tablespoon Ener-G egg replacer

¼ cup (60 ml) warm water

2 cups (250 g) unbleached all-purpose flour

½ teaspoon salt

1 teaspoon baking powder

1 teaspoon ground cassia or cinnamon

½ teaspoon ground nutmeg

¼ to ½ teaspoon turmeric

1 teaspoon vanilla essence, or ½ teaspoon vanilla extract

½ cup (40 g) raisins

¼ cup (28 g) finely grated fresh coconut, optional

2 tablespoons nondairy milk

½ teaspoon Angostura bitters

2 tablespoons granulated sugar

1 teaspoon ground cinnamon

Preheat the oven to 350°F (180°C). Grease a baking sheet.

Put the sugar and shortening in a bowl and cream until fluffy. An electric mixer is helpful here. Whisk the egg replacer and water together, then mix it into the sugar mixture. Add the flour, salt, baking powder, cassia, nutmeg, turmeric, vanilla, raisins, optional coconut, nondairy milk, and bitters. Stir until well combined. The batter should be stiff.

Portion the mixture onto the baking sheet, using about 2 heaping tablespoons of batter for each cake. Bake for 30 minutes, until lightly browned.

Mix the 2 tablespoons granulated sugar and 1 teaspoon cinnamon together in a bag. Add the warm cakes and toss to coat. Serve warm or at room temperature. Store any leftovers in an airtight container.

Eggy Tofu Open-Faced Sandwiches

MAKES ENOUGH FOR 12 MINI OR 6 LARGE OPEN-FACED SANDWICHES

This is one of those recipes that you can make for people who say they do not like tofu. Although I am not the biggest fan of tofu, this is one tofu recipe that I love because it is so full of flavor. If you have black salt or are willing to buy some, use it in this dish; it will give the flavor of boiled eggs.

1½ cups (375 ml) water

2 teaspoons distilled white vinegar

5 ounces (150 g) firm tofu

1 tablespoon minced pickles or celery

1 tablespoon chopped red bell pepper, minced

1 teaspoon minced parsley

⅛ teaspoon minced ginger

1 teaspoon Madras curry powder

½ teaspoon ground cumin

¼ teaspoon salt, preferably black salt

¼ teaspoon mild paprika

¼ teaspoon white pepper

3 tablespoons vegan sour cream

1 tablespoon vegan mayonnaise

1 teaspoon Bajan Pepper Sauce (page 23), optional

⅛ to ¼ teaspoon minced Scotch bonnet or habanero pepper, optional

1 teaspoon mild chiles, such as Hungarian wax peppers, minced, optional

¼ teaspoon chopped fresh marjoram, or ⅛ teaspoon dried, optional

Combine the water and vinegar in a small saucepan over medium heat. Bring to a boil, add the tofu, and cook for 5 minutes. Drain the tofu and let it sit until cool enough to handle.

Crumble the tofu into a bowl. Add the pickles, bell pepper, parsley, ginger, curry powder, cumin, salt, paprika, white pepper, vegan sour cream, and vegan mayonnaise. Stir until well combined. Taste and add the optional pepper sauce, Scotch bonnet, mild chiles, and marjoram as desired. Chill spread before making sandwiches.

 **ISLAND TIP**

When making open-faced sandwiches with this, you can toast the bread or even flatten it with a rolling pin before toasting. Watercress is a traditional garnish for these sandwiches. You could also top the sandwiches with some minced Everyday Vegan "Ham" (page 100) if you like.

Light Sweet Raisin Bread

This bread is reminiscent of a loaf sold in Barbados that is eaten with warm milk. If you do not like raisins, replace them with any candied fruit of your choice. Larger candied fruits should be chopped before they are added. This bread is perfect for breakfast and tea and is excellent warm with margarine.

> **One ¼-ounce package (2½ teaspoons / 7 g) active dry yeast**
> **¼ cup (56 g) granulated sugar**
> **1 cup plus 2 tablespoons (265 ml) warm nondairy milk (110°F to 115°F / 43°C to 46°C)**
> **3½ cups (438 g) unbleached all-purpose flour**
> **½ teaspoon salt**
> **½ cup (115 g) vegan margarine**
> **½ cup (40 g) raisins**
> **½ teaspoon ground cinnamon**
> **½ teaspoon ground cassia or additional cinnamon**
> **¼ teaspoon ground ginger**
> **¼ teaspoon ground nutmeg**
> **½ teaspoon vanilla essence, or ¼ teaspoon vanilla extract**
> **1 teaspoon sugar mixed with 2 tablespoons water**

Stir the yeast and sugar into the nondairy milk and let stand for about 10 to 20 minutes, until the top is foamy. (If the yeast doesn't foam, it's dead or the milk was too hot or too cool. You need to start over with fresh yeast.)

Put the flour and salt in a large bowl. Add the margarine and rub it into the flour with your fingertips or a pastry blender until the mixture resembles fine bread crumbs. Stir in the raisins, cinnamon, cassia, ginger, and nutmeg. Make a well in the center of the flour and pour in the yeast mixture and vanilla essence. Stir until the dough comes together, then knead it in the bowl for about 5 minutes, until the dough is smooth and leaves the side of the bowl clean.

Turn the dough out onto a lightly floured surface and knead for 2 minutes, until fairly smooth. Put the dough in a lightly oiled bowl in a warm, draft-free place, cover, and let rise until doubled in size, about 1 hour in a warm climate or 2½ hours in more temperate regions.

Punch the dough down and let it rise again until almost doubled in size, about 30 minutes in a warm climate or 1¼ hours in more temperate regions.

Lightly grease a 9 x 5-inch (23 x 13 cm) loaf pan. Punch the dough down, form it into a loaf shape, and place it in the prepared pan. Cover and let rise for 30 minutes until it has risen by one-third in size

Preheat the oven to 350°F (180°C).

Brush the top of the loaf with the sugar-water. Bake for about 40 minutes, periodically brushing the top with the sugar-water. The baked loaf should be golden brown.

Cool before slicing and serving.

Coconut Bread

This coconut bread is dense bread and may look dry, but when you eat it the texture is smooth. Because it is vegan and doesn't rely on real eggs, you knead the dough for a long time to develop the gluten, which acts as a binding agent in the bread. In the Caribbean, everyone enjoys coconut bread, from children to workmen on their break. The best occasion for coconut bread is teatime. Coconut bread is quite popular during the holiday seasons, and these loaves make excellent gifts for friends and family.

4½ cups (568 g) unbleached all-purpose flour

1 tablespoon baking powder

1 teaspoon ground cinnamon or cassia

1 teaspoon ground nutmeg

1 cup (200 g) light brown sugar

4 cups (400 g) finely grated fresh coconut, or 3 cups (400 g) frozen grated coconut

1½ teaspoons Ener-G egg replacer

2 tablespoons warm water

⅓ cup plus 1 teaspoon (85 g) vegan margarine

⅓ cup plus 1 teaspoon (85 g) vegetable shortening

1 tablespoon almond essence, or 1½ teaspoons almond extract

1 teaspoon molasses, optional

¾ cup plus 1 tablespoon (188 ml) nondairy milk

⅓ cup (50 g) raisins, chopped candied cherries, or a combination, optional

2 teaspoons sugar dissolved in ¼ cup water

Preheat the oven to 350°F (180°C). Grease and lightly flour two 7½ x 3¾-inch (19 x 10 cm) loaf pans.

Mix the flour, baking powder, cinnamon, nutmeg, and brown sugar together in a large bowl. Add the grated coconut. Mix the egg replacer with the water and add to the flour mixture.

In a small saucepan on the stove top, or in the microwave, melt the margarine and shortening together. Add the almond essence to the melted margarine and shortening. Add the mixture to the flour and stir until evenly combined. Stir the optional molasses into the nondairy milk. Add the milk to the flour mixture, along with the optional fruit. Bring the dough together with your hands. At this stage the dough is very thick but as it is kneaded it will become pliable.

Knead for 15 minutes in the bowl. You should start to see the strands of gluten forming. Turn the dough out on a lightly floured surface, shape the dough into two loaves, and place them in the prepared pans. Bake for about 1 hour, brushing with the sugar-water a few times during the baking process. The baked loaves should be golden brown.

Cool before slicing and serving. The bread can keep at room temperature for as long as 3 days.

 ISLAND TIP

In the Caribbean, people enjoy this bread with a slice of cheese, as I used to before I was vegan, so if you find a good vegan cheddar give it a try. This recipe calls for candied cherries, also known as glace cherries. These are *not* the same as maraschino cherries. Whole wheat coconut bread is also very popular and can be made by using whole wheat flour with 2 tablespoons of gluten flour and an extra 30 minutes of baking at 235°F (113°C).

Jam Buns

The British may call these buns, and Americans will call them cookies, but whatever you call them, they have become one of my top five baked goods to give people during the holidays. They are one of the first things I learned to bake at school. I do not remember them tasting this good, so maybe it is the vegan twist to the recipe. Use whatever jam you like, or a mixture of jams for a stunning presentation. It is best to mix this dough by hand.

> 1 cup (125 g) unbleached all-purpose flour
> ½ cup (113 g) granulated sugar
> 1 teaspoon baking powder
> ¼ teaspoon salt
> ⅓ cup (76 g) vegan margarine
> 1½ teaspoons Ener-G egg replacer
> 2 tablespoons warm water
> 1 teaspoon lemon zest
> ½ cup (125 ml) red fruit jam, or an assortment of jams, for filling your buns
> 2 teaspoons sugar dissolved in ¼ cup water, optional

Preheat the oven to 350°F (180°C). Line a baking sheet with parchment paper.

Mix the flour, sugar, baking powder, and salt together in a bowl. Add the margarine and rub it into the flour with your fingertips or a pastry blender until the mixture resembles crumbs. Whisk the warm water and egg replacer together, then add it to the dough, along with the zest. Stir until evenly incorporated. This dough will be dry, not sticky, but if it's too crumbly to form into small balls, mix in another tablespoon of water.

Divide the dough into 10 equal pieces and roll each into a smooth ball with your hands. Place the balls on the baking sheet and make a 1½-inch (4 cm) indentation in the middle of each. Spoon a scant tablespoon of jam into each indentation.

Bake for 15 to 18 minutes, until done.

Arrowroot Tea Biscuits

MAKES 20 BISCUITS

Arrowroot biscuits are light, flavorful biscuits that I grew up eating as a child. Arrowroot is grown on Saint Vincent and Saint Martin and is used to make arrowroot powder or flour, which are in fact the same product. These are no fuss at all to make.

> **2 cups (250 g) unbleached all-purpose flour**
> **⅔ cup (80 g) arrowroot flour**
> **½ cup (113 g) granulated sugar**
> **1 teaspoon baking powder**
> **½ teaspoon salt**
> **⅓ cup (76 g) vegan margarine**
> **⅓ cup (76 g) vegetable shortening**
> **⅓ cup plus 1 tablespoon (90 ml) water**
> **1 teaspoon vanilla essence, or ½ teaspoon vanilla extract**

Put the flours, sugar, baking powder, and salt in a bowl and stir to combine. Add the margarine and shortening and rub it into the flour with your fingertips or a pastry blender until the mixture resembles bread crumbs. Add the water and vanilla essence and stir until the dough comes together. Cover the dough and refrigerate for 1 hour, which will help ensure the biscuit's crispiness.

Preheat the oven to 350°F (180°C). Line a baking sheet with parchment paper.

Roll the dough out to a thickness of about ¼ inch (6 cm). Cut out 3-inch (8 cm) rounds and place them on the prepared baking sheet. Gather the scraps together, roll them out again, and cut more biscuits. These don't expand too much when they're baked, so they can be placed closely together.

Bake for 11 to 15 minutes, until lightly browned. Cool before serving.

Ginger Tea

A very common way of having this tea in the Caribbean is to serve it with cream. If you can find a good nondairy creamer, try it in this recipe, omitting the lime juice.

1 tablespoon grated ginger
1½ cups (375 ml) water
1 teaspoon fresh lime juice
Island Simple Syrup (page 211), sugar, or agave nectar

Put the ginger and water in a small saucepan and boil for 5 minutes; alternatively, bring the water to a boil, pour it over the ginger, cover, and steep for 30 to 60 minutes. Strain, add the lime juice, and sweeten to taste. Reheat if necessary.

Lemongrass Agave Tisane

On some islands, lemongrass grows wild. When you drive through the countryside on these islands, the smell of lemongrass pervades the atmosphere, which is quite delightful. This tea can also be served cold, as an iced tea.

½ cup lemongrass, chopped
2 cups (250 ml) water
Island Simple Syrup (page 211), sugar, or agave nectar

Put the lemongrass and water in a small saucepan and boil for 5 minutes; alternatively, bring the water to a boil, pour it over the lemongrass, cover, and steep for 30 minutes to 1 hour. Strain, then sweeten to taste. Reheat if necessary.

Thyme Tea

I was introduced to this fragrant tea by a friend in Guadeloupe who lived off the land. Who knew that you could drink thyme?

15 sprigs of dried thyme
2 cups (500 ml) water
Island Simple Syrup (page 211), sugar, or agave nectar

Put the thyme and water in a small saucepan and boil for 5 minutes; alternatively, bring the water to a boil, pour it over the thyme, cover, and steep for 30 minutes to 1 hour. Strain, then sweeten to taste. Reheat if necessary.

Bay Leaf Tea

Either fresh bay leaf or dried works well for this tea but each gives a slightly different flavor. The smell is intoxicating and the taste is unforgettable!

5 dried bay leaves
2 cups (500 ml) water
1 teaspoon nondairy creamer
Island Simple Syrup (page 211), sugar, or agave nectar

Put the bay leaves and water in a small saucepan and boil for 5 minutes. Cover and steep for 1 hour. Stir in the creamer, then sweeten to taste.

Citrus Spiced Tea

I do not experience autumn very often, but this would be the perfect hot beverage for the season. When making this tea, I usually use a mixture of orange, tangerine, and lime peels that I have dried outside for a few days.

1 cup of assorted dried citrus peel

1 cinnamon stick or cassia stick

3 whole cloves

3 cups (750 ml) water

Island Simple Syrup (page 211), sugar, or agave nectar

Put the citrus peel, cinnamon stick, cloves, and water in a small saucepan and boil for 10 minutes. Strain, then sweeten to taste.

Basil Tea

This tea does not taste like basil at all, so do not be skeptical of trying it. Many people in the Caribbean have what we call a kitchen garden, where herbs are planted. When there is an abundance of basil, we use it up in this tea. Something about it reminds me of mint. Basil tea is very popular in Morocco as well, where it is served as a sweet dessert tea in many restaurants.

25 basil leaves on their stems

2½ cups (625 ml) water

Brown sugar, agave nectar, or Island Simple Syrup (page 211)

Put the basil and water in a small saucepan and boil for 10 to 15 minutes. Strain, then sweeten to taste.

8

DESSERTS

I DID NOT eat a lot of dessert when I was growing up because it wasn't something that was served every day. For me, dessert was usually fruit: often golden apples or mangoes. However, we did make desserts in large quantities during the holidays.

One of my fondest childhood memories is of my father multitasking in the kitchen, making coconut bread while mixing up a cake in another bowl. In a matter of hours the kitchen would look like a bakery, with all sorts of cakes and pastries stacked up and covered. The phone would be ringing off the hook because family and friends wanted to put in their orders for bread, as baking appeared to be too much work for some of them. When my dad went vegan, those cakes stopped—for health reasons, and because both of us wondered how we could make cake without eggs. It took about two years for me to finally give vegan baking another thought, and now I have recreated all of the things I used to have for the holidays.

Caribbean desserts are celebratory desserts, and the recipes have been around for a while. Sometimes a chef might come up with something new, but they tend to keep those flavor profiles consistent or to reconstruct an existing dessert. Another interesting fact about Caribbean desserts is that some of them use vegetables instead of fruits; ingredients such as cassava and pumpkin tend to work well in sweet applications like pones or puddings.

When using coconut for desserts, I always say the more finely grated the better, so get out your box grater or food processor. Big pieces of coconut tend not to incorporate well into the desserts in this book, resulting in an unpleasant mouthfeel. Use fresh coconut where possible. If you cannot get fresh coconut, check the frozen section of your supermarket for grated coconut. If you use dried coconut, please note that it needs to be hydrated with a bit of coconut milk. And if you use sweetened dried coconut, you will probably need to reduce the amount of sugar in the recipe, depending on how much sugar and coconut the recipe calls for. The rule is fresh is best, then frozen, then dried.

Desserts containing alcohol show up often all over the Caribbean. I like to use the rum of the island that the dessert comes from. If I cannot find that type of rum, I tend to go for a high-quality rum from the Caribbean. If the rum is not of a good quality, it can result in a bitter taste, especially if the recipe calls for a lot of rum or you add too much. I usually keep rum-soaked raisins at home in a sealed container. The longer you soak them, the juicier and more full of flavor they become. You can use them in many desserts, or as a decoration in clear alcoholic beverages.

Some of our desserts are influenced by more than one culture, and that is something that is unique about Caribbean desserts.

Banana Bread

Banana bread is loved around the world, and this is a moist, no-fail recipe. Make it for your next vegan bake sale or potluck. The secret is the vegan sour cream, so do not substitute anything for it.

1 cup (250 ml) pureed overripe banana (about 3 fresh or frozen bananas)

½ cup (120 g) vegetable shortening

1 tablespoon Ener-G egg replacer

¼ cup (60 ml) warm water

¼ cup (62 ml) vegan sour cream

2 tablespoons nondairy milk

1 tablespoon rum, optional

½ teaspoon vanilla extract

½ teaspoon almond extract

½ teaspoon Angostura bitters

2 cups (250 g) unbleached all-purpose flour

¾ cup (150 g) brown sugar

1 teaspoon baking soda

½ teaspoon salt

½ teaspoon ground cinnamon

Preheat the oven to 350°F (180°C). Grease a 9 x 5-inch (23 x 13 cm) loaf pan.

Put the banana and shortening in a large bowl and beat them together. Whisk the egg replacer and water together, then add it to the bowl. Add the sour cream, nondairy milk, optional rum, vanilla extract, almond extract, bitters, flour, sugar, baking soda, salt, and cinnamon and stir until well combined.

Scrape the batter into the prepared pan and bake for 1 hour, until done. Test with a skewer for doneness or press the top gently and if it springs back it is done.

ISLAND TIP

If you have a lot of bananas, let them get overripe, peel them, and then freeze them whole. They will keep for a long time in the freezer. Later, you can puree them as soon as they have slightly thawed.

Gingerbread

I remember my gingerbread making class at secondary school. We were divided into groups, and each group was required to make three versions: dense, light, and medium in texture. I was stuck with the dense bread and, unfortunately, it did not work out. Fast forward, and now I present to you my version of gingerbread, without the corn syrup that it usually relies on. Feel free to color your gingerbread dark brown with molasses if you have not made the Caribbean Caramel.

2 cups (250 g) unbleached all-purpose flour

¼ cup (20 g) candied citrus peel

¾ cup (150 g) light brown sugar

2 tablespoons finely chopped fresh ginger

2½ teaspoons ground ginger

½ teaspoon salt

¼ teaspoon ground cloves

¼ teaspoon ground cinnamon

⅛ teaspoon ground nutmeg

⅔ cup (167 ml) nondairy milk

1 teaspoon Caribbean Caramel (page 25) or browning

1 tablespoon hot water

1 teaspoon baking soda

¼ cup (57 g) vegan margarine

¼ cup (57 g) vegetable shortening

Preheat the oven to 400°F (200°C). Grease a 9 x 7-inch (23 x 18 cm) loaf pan.

Put the flour, candied citrus peel, sugar, fresh ginger, ground ginger, salt, cloves, cinnamon, nutmeg, nondairy milk, and Caribbean Caramel in a large bowl and stir until well combined. Mix the hot water and baking soda together and stir it into the flour mixture.

Melt the margarine and shortening and stir them into the batter. Scrape the batter into the prepared pan. Bake for 15 minutes, then lower the heat to 350°F (180°C) and bake for 40 minutes, until cooked. Test for doneness by inserting a skewer into the bread. Serve warm.

Barbadian Coconut Turnovers

You are in for a treat with these fluffy yeasted buns. They contain a sweet coconut filling and are baked to perfection with a crispy sugar topping. In Barbados, coconut turnovers are usually consumed on Sundays with a glass of juice or tea. This vegan adaptation tastes just like the real thing—no one would be able to tell the difference. Make them for brunch or for a summer picnic.

One ¼-ounce package (2½ teaspoons / 7 g) active dry yeast

¼ cup (56 g) granulated sugar

1 cup (250 ml) warm nondairy milk (110°F to 115°F / 43°C to 46°C)

3½ cups (438 g) unbleached all-purpose flour

½ teaspoon salt

½ cup (119 g) vegan margarine

2 cups (200 g) finely grated fresh coconut

¾ cup (150 g) light brown sugar

1½ teaspoons almond essence, or ¾ teaspoon almond extract

2 teaspoons sugar dissolved in ¼ cup water

Turbinado sugar

Stir the yeast and granulated sugar into the nondairy milk and let stand for about 15 minutes, until the top is foamy. (If the yeast doesn't foam, it's dead or the milk was too hot or too cool. You need to start over with fresh yeast.)

Put the flour and salt in a large bowl and stir to combine. Add the margarine and rub it into the flour with your fingertips or a pastry blender until the mixture resembles fine bread crumbs. Make a well in the center of the flour and pour in the yeast mixture. Stir until the dough comes together, then knead it in the bowl until the dough is smooth and leaves the side of the bowl clean.

Knead the dough in the bowl for about 5 minutes, until the dough is fairly smooth. Put the dough in a lightly oiled bowl in a warm, draft-free place, cover, and let rise until dough has doubled in size, about 1 hour in a warm climate or 2 hours in more temperate regions.

Mix the coconut, brown sugar, and almond essence together to create the filling. Stir for a few minutes so that the sugar can melt a little and the mixture is a little moist. Set aside.

Divide the dough into 8 equal pieces. Working on a lightly floured surface, roll each piece out to a diameter of 4½ to 5 inches (11 to 13 cm). They should be about ¼-inch

(6 mm) thick. Spoon about 2 to 3 heaping tablespoons of filling into the center of each dough circle. Don't use too much, or you will not be able to seal them and the filling may burst out during baking. Fold each circle in half over the filling, pressing the edges tightly to ensure that the filling stays inside. Bring the two ends together again and squeeze tightly. Form into a miniature loaf shape. (See photo insert, page 9.)

Grease two 7½ x 3¾-inch (19 x 10 cm) loaf pans and place the turnovers in the pans. Put the pans in a warm, draft-free place, cover, and let rise for 30 minutes to 1½ hours, until the turnovers have increased in size by one-third.

Preheat the oven to 350°F (180°C).

Brush the turnovers with the sugar-water, then sprinkle the turbinado sugar over the tops. Bake for 15 minutes, then remove from the oven and brush with the sugar-water again and sprinkle with more turbinado sugar. Bake for an additional 6 to 10 minutes, until tops are golden brown.

Cool slightly and serve warm or at room temperature. They will keep for 1 day at room temperature. After that, refrigerate or freeze them. You can reheat them in the microwave.

 **ISLAND TIP**

Do not use dried coconut in this recipe. Use a mature coconut that has been cracked and grated or frozen grated coconut.

Cassava Pone

Pone is a dessert that's sweet, soft, and almost chewy. It is usually made from vegetables sans flour, instead using the natural starches from the vegetable as binder. When making pone, you must use a very shallow pan. Sometimes this particular pone is eaten with a sprinkle of black pepper or, in many high-end restaurants in Barbados and Tobago, with ice cream made with black pepper. When preparing cassava, you have to grate it so finely that it's almost milky. If it doesn't have a pureed appearance after grating, run it through a food processor. *Caution: Because raw cassava contains a poisonous substance, do not taste the batter!*

3½ tablespoons vegan margarine

3½ tablespoons vegetable shortening, melted

1 tablespoon Ener-G egg replacer

¼ cup (60 g) warm water

3½ cups (770 g) pureed raw cassava

2 cups (200 g) finely grated fresh coconut

1½ cups (338 g) granulated sugar

⅓ cup (50 g) raisins, optional

1¼ cups (313 ml) nondairy creamer or nondairy milk

1½ teaspoons vanilla essence, or ¾ teaspoon vanilla extract

1 teaspoon salt

½ teaspoon ground cinnamon

½ teaspoon ground nutmeg

2 teaspoons sugar dissolved in ¼ cup water

2 teaspoons black pepper, optional

Preheat the oven to 350°F (180°C). Grease a 9 x 7-inch (23 x 18 cm) baking pan.

Melt the margarine and shortening. Whisk the egg replacer and water together. Combine the cassava, coconut, sugar, optional raisins, nondairy creamer, vanilla essence, salt, cinnamon, and nutmeg in a large bowl. Add the melted margarine mixture and egg replacer and stir until well combined. Remember, *do not taste the batter!*

Scrape the batter into the prepared pan and bake for 2 hours, periodically brushing the top of the pone with the sugar-water after the first hour of baking. When fully baked, the pone should be firm to the touch, and the edges should be brown.

When you remove the pone from the oven, sprinkle the pepper over the top if desired. Let the pone cool for 1 hour, then cut it into squares.

ISLAND TIP

For an especially decadent dessert, serve this pone topped with vegan vanilla ice cream sprinkled with black pepper.

Pumpkin Pone

Here is another pone recipe, this time using all things orange. For a perfect fall dessert, serve it topped with crushed pecans and vegan whipped cream or vanilla ice cream.

¼ cup (60 g) vegan margarine

¼ cup (60 g) vegetable shortening

¾ cup (150 g) light brown sugar

1 cup finely grated orange-fleshed sweet potato

1½ cups (320 g) finely grated calabaza squash, or kabocha squash, or any winter squash

1½ cups (150 g) finely grated fresh coconut

⅓ cup (50 g) raisins

1 cup (100 g) fine cornmeal or corn flour

¾ teaspoon salt

1 teaspoon ground nutmeg

1 teaspoon ground allspice

1 cup (250 ml) nondairy creamer or nondairy milk

¼ teaspoon vanilla essence, or ⅛ teaspoon vanilla extract

¼ teaspoon almond essence, or ⅛ teaspoon almond extract

1 teaspoon Angostura bitters, optional

Turbinado sugar

Preheat the oven to 350°F (180°C). Grease a 9 x 7-inch (23 x 18 cm) baking pan.

Melt the margarine and shortening and put them in a bowl. Add the sugar, sweet potato, squash, coconut, raisins, cornmeal, salt, nutmeg, allspice, nondairy creamer, vanilla essence, almond essence, and optional bitters.

Scrape the batter into the prepared pan and bake for 1 hour, until the edges are golden brown, sprinkling the turbinado sugar over the top about 10 minutes before the end of the cooking time. Cool and cut into squares.

Conkies

Conkies, also known as *paime* in Trinidad and Tobago, are pastelles made from a mixture of corn flour, coconut, and pumpkin and steamed in banana leaves. They are a popular traditional food in Barbados and are often eaten around the end of November, as November 30 is our independence day. This is one of those desserts that people make in large quantities and offer to friends and family. Serve them with vegan ice cream if you like. Make sure that the raisins you use are dark and juicy.

Eighteen 8-inch (20 cm) banana leaves or pieces of foil paper lined with wax paper

3 cups (300 g) finely grated fresh coconut (requires roughly 1½ coconuts)

14 ounces (400 g) finely grated calabaza squash or kabocha squash, or any winter squash

9 ounces (260 g) finely grated white-fleshed sweet potato

1¾ cups (340 g) light brown sugar

1 heaping teaspoon salt

1 tablespoon ground cassia or cinnamon

1 teaspoon ground cinnamon

1 tablespoon ground nutmeg

1 cup (250 ml) nondairy milk

2 tablespoons almond essence, or 1 tablespoon almond extract

⅓ cup (80 g) raisins

1 cup (125 g) unbleached all-purpose flour

2 cups (200 g) fine corn flour or fine cornmeal

½ cup (120 g) vegan margarine

¼ cup (57 g) vegetable shortening

If using banana leaves, singe them by passing them over an open flame to make them more pliable.

Put the coconut, squash, sweet potato, sugar, salt, cassia, cinnamon, nutmeg, nondairy milk, almond essence, raisins, flour, and corn flour in a large bowl. Melt the margarine and shortening, add them to the bowl, and stir until thoroughly combined. Set up a steamer, or place about 20 pieces of the center stalk from the banana leaves at the bottom of a large saucepan and barely cover them with water.

Place about ⅓ to ½ cup (83 ml to 125 ml) of the coconut mixture on the ribbed side of a piece of banana leaf (or foil lined with wax paper). Fold along the length of the ribs, bringing the right side of the leaf over to cover the entire conkie mixture, and then folding the left side over in the same way. Fold the other two sides over to form a parcel and secure with kitchen twine.

Steam the conkies for 40 minutes. Check the top conkie for doneness by opening the parcel and testing that the cornmeal is cooked. The conkie should be tender, with all the ingredients well cooked (see photo insert, page 14).

Cool conkies a bit, then serve warm. Store any leftovers in the refrigerator, where they will keep for as long as 3 days, or store them in the freezer for up to 3 months.

Coconut Flan

This is a cold dessert that is set with agar. With its velvet texture and light flavor this is a perfect dessert for a dinner party. Coconut flans are usually offered in restaurants and not usually made at home.

4 cups (500 ml) coconut milk
½ cup (50 g) plus 1 teaspoon granulated sugar
1 teaspoon almond essence, or ½ teaspoon almond extract
½ teaspoon Angostura bitters
¼ teaspoon ground nutmeg
1 tablespoon finely grated fresh coconut, optional
1 to 2 teaspoons agar powder
2 grilled pineapple slices (see Island Tip)
2 candied cherries

Put the coconut milk, sugar, almond essence, bitters, nutmeg, and optional coconut in a heavy saucepan over low heat and bring to a gentle simmer. Increase the heat to medium-low. Add the agar and cook, stirring constantly, for 5 minutes, until it slightly thickens.

Pour the mixture into a two 4-inch (10 cm) ramekins and let cool for 1 hour at room temperature. Cover with plastic and refrigerate for about 2 hours, until completely set, before serving.

To serve, invert the flan onto a plate and garnish the top with the pineapple and cherry.

 **ISLAND TIP**

To grill pineapple slices in the oven, sprinkle a little sugar on a baking sheet and place the pineapple slices on the baking sheet. Dot the pineapple slices with a little vegan margarine and bake at 350°F (180°C) for 25 minutes. The side coated with the sugar in the pan will look as though it was grilled.

Rum Cake

There are two different rum cakes that are commonly made in the Caribbean. There is one that is made during Christmas holidays and for weddings using rum-soaked fruit, called black cake, and then there is one that is made like a regular cake and has a buttered rum glaze, which is this recipe. I was a black cake lover for years until I made this. This cake is perfect for the holidays. It is a crowd-pleaser, and let us not get into how moist it is!

CAKE

¼ cup (62 ml) plus 2 tablespoons dark rum, preferably Mount Gay

¼ cup (62) white rum, or additional dark rum

2 tablespoons falernum (see Island Tip)

½ cup (40 g) raisins

½ cup (113 g) vegan margarine

½ cup (113 g) vegetable shortening

1 cup (200 g) light brown sugar

1 tablespoon Ener-G egg replacer

2 tablespoons warm water

1 teaspoon vanilla essence, or ½ teaspoon vanilla extract

2 cups (250 g) unbleached all-purpose flour

½ teaspoon salt

½ teaspoon baking powder

½ teaspoon baking soda

1 teaspoon ground cinnamon

1 teaspoon apple cider vinegar

1 cup (250 ml) nondairy milk

1 tablespoon molasses

RUM GLAZE

¼ cup (58 g) vegan margarine

3 tablespoon brown sugar

¼ cup (62 ml) water

1 teaspoon vanilla essence, or ½ teaspoon vanilla extract

¼ cup rum, preferably Mount Gay

Pour ¼ cup dark rum, the white rum, and the falernum over the raisins and let it soak overnight or, for many days in a covered container.

Preheat the oven to 350°F (180°C). Grease a 9½ x 3¼-inch (24 x 8 cm) Bundt pan.

Cream the margarine and shortening with the sugar until fluffy using an electric hand mixer. Whisk the egg replacer and water together, then add to the sugar mixture, along with the vanilla essence. Stir vigorously until evenly incorporated. Add the flour, salt, baking powder, baking soda, and cinnamon and mix gently just until incorporated.

Stir the vinegar into milk, then pour the milk into the batter and mix gently. Add the raisins and their soaking liquid, the molasses, and the 2 tablespoons of dark rum and gently fold in these ingredients.

Scrape the batter into the prepared pan and bake for 35 to 40 minutes, until brown. Test for doneness by gently pressing the top of the cake, and if it springs back, it is done.

Meanwhile, make the rum glaze. Combine the margarine, brown sugar, water, and vanilla essence in a small saucepan over low heat. Cook, stirring frequently, until the sugar has dissolved. Turn off the heat and stir in the rum.

Pour the glaze over the cake as it cools. Let the cake cool completely before serving.

ISLAND TIP

Falernum is a flavored syrup that hails from the West Indies. It is full of tropical flavors, including lime and ginger, as well as almond. Look for it in well-stocked liquor stores. For a stunning presentation toss slivered almonds with sugar over medium heat for a few seconds and decorate the cake.

Basic Short Crust Pastry

This pastry works well for pie crusts and patties. It has that melt-in-your-mouth feel typical of short crust. Please review my rules for short crust pastry making (see page 13).

3½ tablespoons vegan margarine

3½ tablespoons vegetable shortening

1½ cups (188 g) unbleached all-purpose flour

¼ teaspoon salt

¼ cup (60 ml) ice-cold water, plus up to 1 tablespoon more

Mix the margarine and shortening lightly, then refrigerate for 20 minutes.

Cut the fat into smaller portions and add it to the flour. Using a pastry blender or your fingers and working quickly and lightly, rub the fat into the flour until the mixture resembles fine bread crumbs. Add the salt. Add the water a tablespoon at a time, mixing only briefly after each addition. Quickly form a ball. Wrap the dough in waxed paper and refrigerate for 30 minutes to 1 hour. Roll out and prepare the dough according to the instructions in the recipe.

 **ISLAND TIP**

To make a sweet short crust pastry, add 1 to 2 teaspoons of sugar and ½ teaspoon of lemon zest or lemon extract to the flour before rubbing in the margarine and shortenting.

Pineapple Tarts

This pastry, which is popular in Guyana, is so easy to make that you will wonder why you never thought it up. It is made by stuffing sweet blended pineapple in short crust pastry.

> **One 20-ounce (565 g) can pineapple slices or chunks, in juice**
> **⅓ cup (75 g) granulated sugar**
> **1 recipe Sweet Short Crust Pastry (page 196; see Island Tip)**
> **2 teaspoons sugar dissolved in ¼ cup water, optional**

Put the pineapple, its juice, and the sugar in a blender or food processor and puree until semi-smooth. Transfer to a saucepan and cook, uncovered, over medium heat, stirring occasionally, for about 20 minutes, until most of the excess water has evaporated and the mixture is thick. Let the mixture cool.

Preheat the oven to 350°F (180°C).

Cut the pastry dough into 3 equal pieces for large tarts or 6 equal pieces for small tarts. Quickly and gently roll the pieces out into disks: three 5-inch (13 cm) disks or six 3½-inch (9 cm) disks. Lightly mark a triangle in the middle of each disk. The triangle should occupy the entire disk (see the illustration below).

Spoon equal amounts of the fruit paste into the middle of each triangle. Fold the tarts into triangles, following the markings on the dough. The center with the fruit filling should be slightly exposed.

Place the tarts on a lined baking sheet and bake for 15 to 20 minutes, until lightly golden brown. For a varnished finish, brush the tarts with the optional sugar-water from time to time during baking.

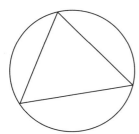

Here is how to mark each disk before filling and folding.

Coconut Tart

This tart shows up in many Caribbean restaurants across the region. I created this vegan version, which is best served cold.

1 recipe Sweet Short Crust Pastry (page 196; see Island Tip)

FILLING

1 cup (250 ml) coconut milk

½ cup (125 ml) nondairy creamer

½ cup (50 g) finely grated fresh coconut

½ cup plus 2 tablespoons (28 g) granulated sugar

1¼ teaspoons grated lime zest

1 teaspoon almond essence, or ½ teaspoon almond extract

3 tablespoons unbleached all-purpose flour

1 tablespoon plus 1 teaspoon arrowroot powder

TOPPINGS

2 tablespoons finely grated fresh coconut

1 teaspoon granulated sugar

10 cherries

Preheat the oven to 400°F (200°C).

Quickly and gently roll out the pastry to a circle with an 8-inch (20 cm) diameter. It should be about ¼-inch (6 mm) thick. Carefully transfer the pastry to an 8-inch (20 cm) tart pan and bake for 17 minutes, then lower the heat to 350°F (180°C) and bake for 5 minutes, until partially cooked.

Meanwhile, put ¾ cup (188 ml) of the coconut milk in a small saucepan over medium heat. Stir in the nondairy creamer, coconut, sugar, lime zest, and almond essence and cook, stirring occasionally, for about 5 minutes, until the mixture comes to a gentle simmer. Whisk in the flour, and continue to cook, whisking constantly, until the mixture begins to thicken. Turn the heat down to low and cook, whisking occasionally, for 2 minutes. Remove from the heat, whisk in the arrowroot powder, and let cool. Stir in the remaining ¼ cup (62 ml) coconut milk.

Pour the mixture into the pastry shell and decorate with the toppings. Sprinkle the coconut and sugar over the filling, then arrange the cherries on top. Bake for 25 to 30 minutes, until lightly browned on top. Cool to room temperature, then refrigerate overnight, until set, before slicing and serving.

 **ISLAND TIP**

Don't substitute cornstarch for the arrowroot powder. It will affect the texture of filling significantly. Remember, when baking pie shells "blind," or without filling, line the pastry with parchment paper and fill the pie well with dried beans.

Rummy Rum and Raisin Ice Cream

MAKES ABOUT 1 QUART (APPROX. 1 LITER)

Rum and raisin ice cream is popular in the countries that make their own rum—go figure. There is something about the strong, robust flavor of sugarcane and the sweetness of the raisins. Do try to soak your raisins for a few days in advance. Barbados, Guadeloupe, Curacao, Jamaica, Trinidad and Tobago, and Guyana all make excellent rums, but I myself have found I most prefer this made with Mount Gay Rum.

½ cup (125 ml) Mount Gay Rum
⅓ cup (83 ml) falernum
2 tablespoons white rum
⅓ cup (50 g) raisins
1 tablespoon plus 1 teaspoon arrowroot powder
1½ cups (375 ml) plus 2 tablespoons (405 ml) nondairy milk
½ cup (100 g) brown sugar
¼ teaspoon ground cloves
¼ teaspoon ground cinnamon
⅛ teaspoon ground allspice, optional
1 tablespoon vegan margarine
1 cup (250 ml) nondairy creamer

Pour ¼ cup of the dark rum, the falernum, and the white rum over the raisins. Hopefully you are doing this in advance and can let them soak for a few days.

Put the 1½ cups nondairy milk and the sugar in a saucepan over low heat and cook, stirring occasionally, until the mixture begins to steam. Stir in the cloves, cinnamon, optional allspice, and margarine. Stir in the nondairy creamer and let the mixture come to a low simmer. Whisk the arrowroot powder into the 2 tablespoons of nondairy milk. Remove the milk and sugar mixture from the heat, immediately stir in the arrowroot powder mixture, and keep stirring until mixture begins to thicken. Chill the mixture thoroughly.

Freeze the mixture in your ice cream maker according to the manufacturer's instructions. During the last 5 minutes of freezing, add the raisins, their soaking liquid, and the remaining ¼ cup dark rum.

☀ ISLAND TIP

Falernum is a flavored syrup that hails from the West Indies. It is full of tropical flavors, including lime and ginger, as well as almond. Look for it in well-stocked liquor stores. Due to the alcohol in the recipe, this ice cream tends to be easily scoopable even after extended freezing.

Piña Colada Ice Cream

What could possibly be better than a tall, cold piña colada? Piña Colada Ice Cream!

2 tablespoons arrowroot powder

½ cup (125 ml) plus 2 tablespoons nondairy milk

1¼ cups (313 ml) coconut milk

1 cup (250 ml) nondairy creamer

1 cup (225 g) granulated sugar

½ cup (125 ml) crushed pineapple

7 candied cherries, finely chopped

½ cup (125 ml) white rum

1 tablespoon coconut essence, or 1½ teaspoons coconut extract, optional

¼ teaspoon Angostura bitters

Whisk the arrowroot powder into the 2 tablespoons of nondairy milk. Put the coconut milk, nondairy creamer, sugar, and the ½ cup nondairy milk in a saucepan over medium-low heat and cook, stirring occasionally. When the mixture begins to boil, remove from heat, stir in the arrowroot mixture, and keep stirring until the mixture starts to thicken.

Let the mixture cool for 1 hour at room temperature, then refrigerate overnight. Do not cheat on this step, as it is very important for getting a creamy texture in the finished product.

Stir in the pineapple, cherries, rum, optional coconut essence, and bitters. Freeze in your ice cream maker according to the manufacturer's instructions. Put the processed ice cream in the freezer for 3 hours, then take it out and stir briskly until the texture is homogenous. Return the ice cream to the freezer and freeze for at least 5 more hours before serving.

ISLAND TIP

 alcohol in the recipe, this ice cream tends to be easily scoopable even after extended freezing.

Soursop Ice Cream

One of the best things about soursop is its thick consistency, which makes it great for ice cream. The fresh juice has a thick consistency on its own, so a light nondairy milk like almond milk works best when making this recipe.

> **1½ tablespoons arrowroot powder**
>
> **1 cup (250 ml) plus 3 tablespoons (45 ml) almond milk**
>
> **2 cups (250 ml) rice or soy creamer**
>
> **½ to ¾ cup (63 g to 94 g) confectioners' sugar**
>
> **1 cup (250 ml) soursop juice**
>
> **1 teaspoon vanilla essence, or ½ teaspoon vanilla extract**

Whisk the arrowroot powder into the 3 tablespoon of nondairy milk. Combine the 1 cup nondairy milk, creamer, and sugar in a saucepan, whisking to combine. Place the mixture over medium-low heat and bring to a simmer, whisking occasionally. Turn the heat down to low and whisk in the arrowroot mixture. Keep whisking until the mixture gets fairly thick. Remove from the heat and stir in the soursop juice and vanilla essence. Cool this mixture for one hour, then refrigerate overnight.

Freeze the mixture in your ice cream maker according to the manufacturer's instructions. Once it's processed, you can serve it right away, but it will be soft; or freeze for 6 hours for a harder consistency.

Tamarind Balls

MAKES ABOUT 6 BALLS

One of my favorite childhood memories is of going to pick tamarinds with my mother in the late 1980s. Usually the trees were very tall, so to get tamarinds my mom and her friends would throw rocks into the trees—after securing the kids far away. Once the rocks had been accounted for, we would scramble under the trees and gather the pods. Back at the house, my mom would make many tamarind balls and store them in a jar. I would think about them every day until they were all gone. Tamarinds are acidic and stimulate the appetite. I also use them to settle an upset stomach. The tamarinds sold in colored boxes from Asia are sweet and are not suitable for preparing this way. You may be able to find the more acidic tamarinds in Spanish markets, where they are often called *tamarindos*.

> **15 tamarind pods, shelled**
> **½ cup (100 g) light brown sugar**
> **Pinch of black pepper**
> **¼ teaspoon Bajan Pepper Sauce (page 23), or ⅛ teaspoon cayenne pepper**

Shell the tamarinds by using tongs to pull the flesh out of the shell. Grab a few pieces of the flesh, with the seed still inside, and press the mass into the sugar until a lot of sugar is incorporated into the flesh. Continue in this way for all of the flesh. Sprinkle the black pepper and pepper sauce over the entire mass. Coat your hands in sugar and roll the tamarind into grape-sized balls.

Store in an airtight container. At room temperature, they will keep for as long as 1 month. Stored in the fridge, they will keep for up to one year.

ISLAND TIP

To eat a tamarind or tamarind ball, take a section of the sweet inclusive of the seed, put it into your mouth, suck off the flesh from the seed, and spit out the seed. The chewy membrane around the seed can also be detached with your teeth and consumed.

Gooseberry Syrup

This syrup can be eaten as is, used to top ice cream, or stirred into oatmeal. If you cannot obtain gooseberries, you can make this recipe with orange zest or any tart fruit of your choice. The beauty of this syrup is that it can also be served as an alternative to maple syrup for topping pancakes.

> **3 cups (600 g) brown sugar**
> **2½ cups (625 ml) water**
> **1 teaspoon ground cinnamon, or 2 cinnamon sticks**
> **½ teaspoon ground nutmeg**
> **¼ teaspoon ground cloves**
> **4 pounds (1.8 kg) gooseberries**

Put the sugar, water, cinnamon, nutmeg, and cloves in a large saucepan over medium heat and bring to a simmer, stirring occasionally. Lower the heat and simmer for 15 to 20 minutes.

Meanwhile, put the gooseberries in a pot of room temperature water and set to boil over high heat. Immediately remove from the heat and drain. This ruptures the skins of the gooseberries, leaving them wrinkled and making it easier for the syrup to penetrate.

Add the gooseberries to the syrup and simmer for 1 hour over low heat. The color of the gooseberries will change from green to red.

Sugar Cakes

This is a common sweet made with coconut and sugar sold in the streets and in gift shops on many islands.

½ cup (125 ml) water
2 cups brown sugar
9 ounces (255 g) finely grated fresh coconut
1 teaspoon almond essence, or ½ teaspoon almond extract
Food coloring, optional

Lightly grease a baking sheet.

Put the water and sugar in a heavy saucepan over medium-high heat and cook, stirring, until the sugar is dissolved. Stir in the coconut and almond essence. Continue to cook over medium-high heat, stirring periodically, for 11 minutes exactly. If using food coloring, add it in quickly as soon as you take the coconut mixture off the heat. At this stage all of the water should have evaporated.

Spoon the mixture onto the baking sheet, using about 2 heaping tablespoon for medium-size cakes or 1 heaping tablespoon for miniature cakes. Leave at room temperature until the cakes set. If you've done a good job, this should take about 15 minutes. Otherwise, it will set overnight. Store the cakes in an airtight container.

ISLAND TIP

For a nice variation, you can add a bit of molasses and bay leaf. Just stir 2 tablespoons molasses and 1 tablespoon crushed bay leaves into the mixture after you add the coconut. Alternatively, you can use 6 whole bay leaves, adding them along with the coconut. Stir gently to keep the bay leaves intact.

Nut Cake

In the Caribbean, some of our peanut brittle recipes are not glassy. Rather, they are fudgelike, as in this recipe. This nut cake is usually sold by sweets vendors, and is good for holiday gift giving. You need a candy thermometer to ensure good results when you make this.

> **2½ cups (500 g) light brown sugar**
> **¾ cup (188 ml) nondairy milk**
> **¼ cup (62 ml) nondairy creamer**
> **2 tablespoons vegan margarine**
> **1 teaspoon vanilla essence, or ½ teaspoon vanilla extract**
> **2 tablespoons chopped ginger, optional**
> **1 teaspoon ground cinnamon or cassia**
> **½ teaspoon salt, optional (only needed if the nuts are unsalted)**
> **2 cups (260 g) peanuts or other nuts**

Grease a baking sheet. Have a glass of ice-cold water standing by in the fridge.

Put the sugar, nondairy milk, nondairy creamer, margarine, vanilla essence, optional ginger, cinnamon, and salt, if needed, in a heavy saucepan over medium-low heat. Cook, stirring constantly, until the sugar starts to dissolve. Increase the heat slightly and continue stirring. At this stage, the mixture will start to bubble and rise up in the saucepan. As the bubbles rise, stir quickly to beat them down. When the temperature starts to approach 236°F (113°C), take a small spoonful of the mixture and drop it into the glass of ice-cold water. If the mixture forms a soft ball upon contact with the water, it will set. Check the temperature again, making sure it is exactly 236°F (113°C). Stir in the nuts and quickly remove mixture from the heat.

Pour the mixture onto the prepared baking sheet and spread to a thickness of 1½ inches (4 cm). Leave at room temperature until set. It should take up to 2 hours to completely set, but it may set in as little as 30 minutes. Break into pieces before serving.

 **ISLAND TIP**

If you do not like ginger, leave it out. You are not restricted to peanuts with this brittle; feel free to use hazelnuts, almonds, or walnuts instead.

9

DRINKS AND COCKTAILS

I COULD NOT write this book without including drinks, punches, and a cocktail or two. In this section you will find some beverages that you can make without too many hard-to-find ingredients. Okay, I admit there at least two things you may have to run around the block (or two) to find, but most drinks in this section are everyday pantry friendly. I have excluded tropical fruit punches because the fruits that I would use for these recipes may be out of season or unavailable where you live.

When making drinks, I tend to use a simple syrup rather than agave nectar, as the syrup works better in here, as it dissolves more easily, especially in alcoholic beverages—and you do not have the raw sugar taste in the drink. It is best to chill all of these drinks before serving, rather than serving them over ice, as that will water them down and diminish the flavor. Starting with cold ingredients will speed the chilling process.

Garnishes are important and festive, especially at parties. Try to think of simple, appropriate garnishes that your guests will enjoy. For example, try using sugarcane sticks or long pieces of fruit as stirrers in rum punch. Shaved chocolate and chopped nuts give a stunning presentation. Another option is splashing some Angostura bitters into the mixed drink.

Please remember to drink responsibly.

Island Simple Syrup

When mixing alcoholic drinks, sugar takes a long time to dissolve. The solution is to use a simple syrup. This sweetens without the problem of undissolved sugar in the drink. Simple syrup is usually made with granulated sugar. I like to make mine with brown sugar so it has some character. The flavor of brown sugar is richer than the granulated sugar and this is what sometimes gives Caribbean cocktails their unique taste.

2 cups (400 g) brown sugar
¾ cup (188 ml) water

Put the sugar and water in a saucepan over low heat and cook, stirring occasionally, until dissolved. Increase the heat to medium-high and bring to a rapid boil, stirring constantly. After 2 minutes of boiling, remove from heat and let cool. Transfer to a clean jar, seal, and refrigerate. The syrup will keep for 6 to 8 months in the fridge.

ISLAND TIP

If you want to sweeten light-colored drinks and worry that the dark syrup will affect the color, use granulated white sugar to make the syrup. Simple syrup sometimes recrystallizes. If this happens, reheat it on the stove or in the microwave and stir until re-dissolved.

You can make many other syrups this way, such as ginger, using fresh ginger syrup, or spiced syrup, using cinnamon sticks and whole cloves. These spices can be added while the syrup cooks. When the syrup has cooled, strain to remove the solids and place in a clean jar or bottle.

Caribbean Lemonade

In the Caribbean we have lemon trees, but there are far more lime trees. Therefore, our lemonade is made with limes and a few drops of bitters, which gives it its yellow-brown color. On a hot day, this is just what you need.

¼ cup (62 ml) fresh lime juice
2½ cups (625 ml) ice-cold water
½ teaspoon Angostura bitters
Island Simple Syrup (page 211) or agave nectar

Mix the lime juice, water, and bitters together, then sweeten to taste. Serve well chilled.

Mauby

A stocky, well-dressed woman sells mauby in the bustle of the city as horse-drawn carriages go by, almost fifty years ago. She sells the mauby from a canister balanced on her head, and when she pours the customer the beastly cold drink, not a drop of mauby gets on her. Perfection! Mauby has been around a long time. It is a drink made from the bark of the mauby tree, a type of buckthorn. This beverage is well suited to the heat, as it is sweet and then very bitter. I never liked mauby when I was growing up because it is so bitter, but now I always stock up on bark when I go home. If you cannot find the bark and want to try mauby, check with your local ethnic market for mauby syrup, mauby concentrate, or mauby bitters. Mixed essence is a flavoring that includes vanilla, almond, and pear flavors.

CONCENTRATE

¾ cup mauby bark

6 cups (1.5 liters) water

10 whole cloves

1 cinnamon stick or cassia stick

½ teaspoon ground cinnamon, if you used a cassia stick

FOR MIXING MAUBY

Island Simple Syrup (page 211) or brown sugar

Mixed essence

Angostura bitters

To make the concentrate, combine the mauby bark and water in a saucepan and boil, uncovered, for 40 minutes. Halfway through the boiling process, add the cloves, cinnamon stick, and ground cinnamon, if using. Turn off the heat and let cool to room temperature.

Strain, transfer to a clean glass or plastic container, seal, and refrigerate overnight before using.

What you now have is a highly concentrated starting material that is too strong and bitter to consume. It will keep for as long as 1 week in the fridge.

To make mauby for two, mix ¼ cup concentrate with 1 cup chilled water. Add enough simple syrup to sweeten, along with 1 tablespoon mixed essence and a few drops of bitters. Serve well chilled.

ISLAND TIP

You need to sweeten the mauby to suit your taste. I use about ¼ cup of sugar when I am making this at home, as I like my Mauby very bitter and less sweet.

Sorrel Drink

In the Caribbean, *sorrel* refers to hibiscus. During the December holidays, drinks and cocktails made from sorrel are traditional, along with ginger beer. Sorrel is a drink that most people will like, so why not shake things up with some white rum? Then you will have yourself a cocktail. Sorrel can be also consumed as a hot beverage. This recipe was developed with dried sorrel, which can be found in most ethnic markets year-round.

CONCENTRATE
1 cup dried sorrel
One 5 x 1-inch (13 cm x 2.5 cm) piece of orange or tangerine peel
⅔ cup (134 g) brown sugar
12 whole cloves
1 teaspoon ground ginger
5¼ cups (1.25 liters) boiling water
1 tablespoon fresh lime juice

FOR MIXING SORREL
Island Simple Syrup (page 211)

To make the concentrate, put the sorrel, orange peel, sugar, cloves, and ginger in a large stainless steel or glass bowl. Pour in the boiling water, cover with a tea towel, and steep for 2 hours.

Strain the concentrate. Stir in the lime juice. Transfer to a clean glass container, seal, and refrigerate. What you now have is a concentrate that you can use to make a sorrel beverage. It will keep for as long as 1 week in the fridge.

To serve sorrel, mix ¾ parts concentrate to 1 part cold water and sweeten with simple syrup to taste.

Fermented Ginger Beer

Ginger beer is a very popular West Indian drink usually consumed during the Christmas period. On some islands, ginger beer is usually fermented. On others, they make a ginger beer that is more like iced tea. This ginger beer is fermented and needs to rest in the kitchen or a warm area for a couple of days. If you are interested in making this in the winter months, you can keep it near a heater. This ginger beer takes up to five days to make, but very little of that is hands-on time. You'll need a 1.5-liter plastic bottle with a secure top for making this.

¼ cup (100 g) coarsely grated or crushed ginger
5¼ cups (1.25 liters) hot water
1 teaspoon active dry yeast
2 teaspoons unbleached all-purpose flour
3½ tablespoons warm water
¾ cup (150 g) brown sugar
¼ cup (62 ml) fresh lime juice
Four 3 x 3-inch (8 cm x 8 cm) pieces of lime peel

Put the ginger in a large metal or glass bowl. Pour in the hot water and stir with a clean spoon. Cover with a tea towel and let stand until the temperature has come down to 86°F (30°C).

Stir the yeast, flour, and warm water together and let stand for a few minutes, until slightly frothy. Stir the yeast mixture into the ginger mixture, along with the sugar, lime juice, and lime peel. Cover with a tea towel and store in a warm, draft-free place.

For the next 3 days, stir twice a day. You will hear a fizzy, popping sound every time you stir. Do not taste the ginger beer until the end of the process.

On the fourth day, strain the ginger beer, then transfer it into a 1.5-liter plastic bottle with a secure lid. Screw on the top and store at room temperature overnight. The bottom of the bottle will swell, as the fermentation reaction is continuing.

The following day, carefully unscrew the top, let the gas out, and push in the bottom of the bottle. Refrigerate to stop the fermentation. Serve well chilled—as is or diluted with cold water.

ISLAND TIP

If you like alcoholic drinks, mix in some dark rum. If you want to increase the alcoholic content of the ginger beer, use about one part rum to four parts ginger beer.

Unfermented Ginger Beer

I grew up drinking this nonalcoholic version of Ginger Beer. The flavor is slightly milder than the fermented version but this beverage can be consumed within 2 days.

3 tablespoons grated ginger
8 cups (2 liters) boiling water
Island Simple Syrup (page 211)

Place the ginger in a large bowl. Pour in the boiling water and stir with a clean spoon. Cover with a tea towel and leave undisturbed for 2 days. Strain, then sweeten with simple syrup to taste. Transfer to a bottle and chill well before serving.

Soursop Punch

Soursop, or guanabana, is a large tropical fruit, and also the name of a very popular drink in the West Indies. The fruit, which has a prickly skin, can be eaten as is, but most people tend to use it to make tarts, ice creams, and beverages. Because the juice from the soursop is very thick, it is suitable for making ice cream. My father helped me develop this recipe, and he suggests a vanilla-flavored nondairy milk. You can substitute store-bought guanabana nectar for the soursop juice in this recipe.

3 cups (250 ml) concentrated soursop juice
1½ cups (375 ml) nondairy milk
¾ cup (55 g) granulated sugar
1 teaspoon vanilla essence, or ½ teaspoon vanilla extract, optional

Combine all of the ingredients. Serve well chilled.

Sea Moss Punch

In many parts of the world, sea moss is known as Irish moss, but in the Caribbean we call it sea moss. Another name for this sea vegetable is carrageen. Known as an aphrodisiac and also touted as a sexual stimulant for men, it is also used to make a punch that is popular over the Caribbean. I always avoided it as a child because of the name and maybe its association with sex—who knows what was going on in my brain at that tender age! My father helped me develop this recipe. The finished product will be a creamy milkshake-like drink infused with island spices. Before we get to the recipe, you should know that the color of the final product may vary. If you use bay leaf, the drink will turn slightly brown, but if you leave it out, you'll sacrifice the nice bay leaf flavor. Also, you need to soak the sea moss overnight before making the punch, so plan ahead.

> **3 ounces (85 g) sea moss, soaked overnight and drained**
> **12¾ cups (3 liters) water**
> **½ teaspoon ground nutmeg**
> **½ teaspoon ground cinnamon or cassia**
> **3 bay leaves, optional**
> **3 cups (750 ml) nondairy milk**
> **½ cup (113 g) granulated sugar**
> **½ teaspoon almond extract**

Combine the sea moss, water, nutmeg, cinnamon, and optional bay leaves in a large pot over high heat and bring to a boil. Turn the heat down to medium-low and cook, uncovered, for 30 to 40 minutes. The liquid should thicken, and most of the sea moss should dissolve. Let cool to room temperature.

Working in batches, blend the mixture until smooth. Stir in the nondairy milk, sugar, and almond extract. Taste and add more sugar if you like. Serve well chilled.

☀ ISLAND TIP

 this punch to make vegan sea moss ice cream. Just put the punch into an ice cream maker and proceed according to the manufacturer's instructions.

Coconut Punch

A good coconut punch always starts with grating a coconut and making milk from the flesh. What happens next is the chef's preference. This thick beverage can be frozen to make blocks of sorbet (see Island Tip).

> **Flesh of 1 coconut, finely grated**
> **1 cup (250 ml) water**
> **2 cups (500 ml) nondairy milk**
> **1 tablespoon almond essence, or 1½ teaspoons almond extract**
> **½ cup (113 g) granulated sugar**
> **¼ teaspoon ground cinnamon or cassia**
> **¼ teaspoon ground nutmeg**

Mix the grated coconut and water together in a bowl. With clean hands, squeeze the coconut flesh to extract some of the milk from the flesh. Stir in the nondairy milk, essence, sugar, cinnamon, and nutmeg. Transfer the mixture to a blender and blend for 30 seconds, until well mixed. Strain and serve well chilled.

 ISLAND TIP

You can use this punch to make cubes of sorbet. Add a few drops of food coloring if you like; you can make several small batches in different colors. Pour the mixture into an ice tray and freeze. These colorful frozen cubes are called ice cream blocks and are a traditional frozen dessert that was once sold in the streets.

Peanut Punch

This peanut punch is inspired by a tiny juice bar called JNC in Barbados, in the Sheraton Centre mall. It serves up the best peanut punch I have ever had. Every time I go home, I have to get a peanut punch there. Although I don't know JNC's recipe, I used my supersensitive taste buds to come up with this version, and it is close to the one sold there.

 2 cups (500 ml) nondairy milk
 ⅓ cup (115 g) creamy peanut butter
 2 tablespoons agave nectar
 ½ teaspoon brewer's yeast
 ¼ teaspoon nutmeg, freshly grated
 ½ teaspoon ground cinnamon
 ¼ teaspoon ground cinnamon or cassia

Put all of the ingredients in a blender. Blend for 1 minute, until smooth. Serve well chilled.

 **ISLAND TIP**

You can add peanuts to this punch, but you will need a powerful blender. You can also add 1 tablespoon of protein powder to enhance the nutritional value; if you do, increase the amount of agave nectar by 1 teaspoon. Brewer's yeast, the nutritional supplement, should not be confused with nutritional yeast flakes. You should be able to find brewer's yeast in most health food stores.

Rum Punch

I fell in love with rum punch one night when I was on vacation in Guadeloupe and vowed to make one of my own that was simple but unique. This is what I came up with. Similar rum punches are found on many islands. I like to make mine with a mixture of pineapple and orange juice, but you could also use passion fruit juice.

1 cup (250 ml) fresh orange juice

1 cup (250 ml) pineapple juice

½ cup (125 ml) Mount Gay Rum

2 tablespoons sugar or Island Simple Syrup (page 211)

2 teaspoons fresh lime juice

1 teaspoon Angostura bitters

Combine all of the ingredients. Serve well chilled.

ISLAND TIP

Do not skimp on the bitters, as this ingredient makes the cocktail come alive. Use fine-quality orange and pineapple juices that you would enjoy drinking on their own, not cheap, artificially flavored varieties.

ACKNOWLEDGMENTS

I COULD NOT have written this book without some amazing people behind me. In a list of no particular order of ranking, I present to you my dream team.

- Cecelia Sonson, my mother, who brought me into this world and told me to go after what I want in life every day. She also worked very hard when I returned home for the photo shoot. Thank you for cleaning up my mess and my future messes. I love you, Mom.
- Laurent Guillaume, husband and friend, who ate all 125 recipes in this book without gaining a pound. Tell me your secret, please.
- Cynthia Nelson, friend, mentor, and photographer. Thank you for offering your services in all of the aforementioned positions, and doing it with such grace and without getting too frustrated with my demands. You have helped me in so many ways.
- Michelle "Bajangyal" Eastmond, my first fan and biggest critic to date. You were there encouraging me to go on writing my blogs and following through with my dreams, even before the idea for the book came up.
- Sunita Jones, university in Barbados was working you hard, but you ran out to get me a tawa and cou-cou stick when I had given up hope on finding them. Thank you for being there and for editing my work when you were doing your thesis at the same time. I hope to return the favor one day.
- Ricardo Mason, my father and kitchen archenemy—and major cooking influence in my life. You were there for everything from turnover competitions in Toronto to helping me with my photo shoot when I returned home, and also donating a few recipes to this book. Thank you, Dad. You are the reason I can cook this good.

- Philomene Sonson, aka Mummy, my grandmother. Even if the cold is beating you up in Ontario, it doesn't stop you from running to the Asian grocery every day to get your ground provisions. From cassava flour and avocado to Saint Lucian Bakes, you may not have known you were teaching me to love your food and your culture, but you were.
- Constanze Reichardt, one of my earlier testers who put her excellent bread-making skills to some of the recipes in the book.
- Nicole Gibs, a new friend I met in Saint Martin. Thank you for dumping off loads of gooseberries and whatever fruits your mom had in the garden, and for taking care of Ti'moune when I had to travel.
- Jocelyn Kimmel, who tested for me. Even when life went wrong for you, you came back strong and tested some more—and you gave me the prettiest baras I ever saw, even if they were colored green with the wrong split pea flour but hey, now we can warn others. You did me proud and showed you are a good friend. Cheers for Jocelyn and her grandma.
- Kirsten Lakso, who tested most of the core recipes in this book, even if I wasn't totally ready. This woman could cook circles around me. Thank you for your help.
- Elizabeth Carls, Miss Banana Bread. Thank you for doing most of the sweets and helping me out when the French baking pans I had would not cooperate with me.
- Allysia Kerney and Logan, I would like to thank both of you for testing and tasting, and also offer a special mention to band members for sending feedback on the dishes.
- Dennis Martinez and wife, thanks again for your support and pictorial feedback on the dishes you tested.
- Liz Wyman, thank you for chatting with me during the good and the bad times and for always giving me feedback. I am glad you learned that Caribbean food is fun, and keep watching Gary Rhodes shows. If I get rich I will send you a box of Jamaican ackee.
- Miriam Griffin, thanks to you and your family and friends for testing and tasting my recipes. Your work is greatly appreciated.
- Dayna Rozental, Miss Ethnic Supermarket Lover, who tested most of the drinks in this book. You surprised me and showed me that there is nothing that can't be found in a big city. Thank you so much.
- Jamie Coble, thank you for coming on board with the testing, and for your dedication and honest feedback.
- Dawne Eng, I want to thank you for doing a lot of the testing when I was just starting out. I wish you success in your future endeavors.

- Winnie Smith, I cannot begin to thank you for all of the testing you did, especially with your schedule. You did an excellent job and I really appreciate you taking the time to test for the book.
- Danielle Jo Bays, I love your honesty and your dedication to this project.
- Tiffany Cadiz, although you were the last to join the group of testers, you put in a lot of work and that amazed me. Thank you for helping me.
- Matthew Lore, publisher of The Experiment. You said yes to me when many other people would have said no. Thank you for taking a chance with me.
- Jennifer Beans Figz and Katz Soloman, your enthusiasm and dedication will never be forgotten, not to mention your constant updates on your blog. Thank you.
- Zsuzsa Nemeth, you made me proud. Even if you were short on time, you worked very hard. A special thanks to you and your husband for testing and tasting for me.
- Jenny Howard, thank you for your support and testing efforts.
- Serenity, thank you so much for testing and giving your honest take on each recipe. I definitely will not forget you.
- Felix Padilla, thanks for giving tips about Trinidadian cuisine. You are such an inspiration.
- Felicity Moon, thank you for your help and for putting the experiences on your blog.
- To all I did not mention, I want to thank you for helping this project become a reality.

INDEX

Note: 📷 indicates that the recipe is pictured in the photo insert.

ABOUT THE AUTHOR

TAYMER MASON grew up in a family of cooks who taught her to make—and love!—traditional Caribbean cuisine. She went vegan in 2006 while an undergraduate at the University of the West Indies and discovered that, far from being limiting, it was an exciting new way to cook her old favorites. Now she writes the popular cooking blog Vegan in the Sun (caribbeanvegan.wordpress.com). She lives with her husband and their cat in the French West Indies, but she appreciates the unique culture and cuisine of all the islands—and especially of her birthplace, Barbados.